Aifreann na hÉireann

Aifreann na hÉireann

The Holy Mass According to the Lorrha Missal

Dustin A. Ashley

RESOURCE *Publications* • Eugene, Oregon

AIFREANN NA HÉIREANN
The Holy Mass According to the Lorrha Missal

Resource Publications
An Imprint of Wipf and Stock Publishers
199 W. 8th Ave., Suite 3
Eugene, OR 97401

www.wipfandstock.com

PAPERBACK ISBN: 979-8-3852-3569-8
HARDCOVER ISBN: 979-8-3852-3570-4
EBOOK ISBN: 979-8-3852-3571-1

12/02/24

May he who has written this book and the one for whom this book has been written for be healthy. Amen.

Contents

Acknowledgments

THIS BOOK IS A PROJECT that has taken years of long nights and arduous labor to bring into fruition. If it wasn't for my amazing support group, namely my professors, colleagues, friends, and family, then this project would have been another idea to emerge and be quickly forgotten.

I thank the late Theresa Monica Cross for her encouragement to begin this project. While we never met in person, this book would not exist without her input and desire to see a complete and authentic Gaelic Rite.

I thank Fr. Robert Gillispie for offering his advice and consultation during the editing process. His insights and experience in Orthodox liturgy was foundational in forming the liturgical material contained herein.

I thank Rev. Brent Williams for offering his support and encouragement in this project, as I hope that this book further aids in materializing a strong and vibrant Gaelic community within southwestern Virginia.

I wish to thank all the professors and scholars I have encountered throughout this project, who have offered their input to ensure a high standard of quality is present within this book.

I thank the Matthew Wimer, George Callihan, Joe Delahanty, Calvin Jaffarian, and all the people at Wipf and Stock who have been a great help in making this book accessible to all interested in the liturgical practices of the early Irish church.

Introduction

CHRISTIAN LITURGY CONSISTS OF two parts: the Liturgy of the Catechumens and Liturgy of the Faithful. The Liturgy of the Word—referred to as the *synaxis* in the Eastern tradition and *collecta* in the Western tradition—is a Christianization of the synagogue service and consists of a series of prayers, psalms, and readings appointed for the day. The Liturgy of the Faithful, also known as the *Eucharist* or "Lord's Supper,"[1] commemorates the Last Supper and serves as the central point of Christian worship.

As various cultures adopted the Christian faith, their culture and language served as a means of interpretation. The earliest liturgical text is the *Didache*, dated to around the first century AD, which contained Church Orders pertaining to baptism, Eucharist, church organization, and Christian ethics. The text served as the foundation for the development of liturgical traditions throughout the various church traditions.

This resulted in the development of various liturgical traditions, formed from the cultural interpretation of Christian worship around the principles present in the *Didache*. Within the first centuries, the Western churches developed the Eucharistic service into the Mass (*missa*) while the Eastern churches developed it into the Divine Liturgy (*litourgia*). Throughout the Western churches, various rites emerged including the Ambrosian Rite celebrated in Milan, the Iberian Mozarabic Rite, and Gallican Rite found in Roman Gaul.[2]

Noted for its diverse assortment of liturgical rites and reportedly ornate plainchant, the Gallican Rite includes texts such as the

---

1. 1 Cor. 11:20–21
2. See Heller and Lamparter, "Worship and Spirituality," 339.

xi

Missale Gothicum, *Missale Francorum*, Bobbio Missal, and Lectionary of Luxeuil.[3] While none of these texts emerge earlier than the 7th century, the letters of St. Germain of Paris are dated to the 6th century and offer descriptions of an earlier liturgical practice.

The Gallican Rite was gradually Romanized, where evidence of this process is found in the Gelasian Sacramentary, an 8th century liturgical text spuriously attributed to the 5th century Pope Gelasius. The degree of liturgical diversity also created a desire for a more uniform Rite celebrated within medieval Europe, beginning with local councils such as those held in Vannes, Agde, Vaison, Tours, Auxerre, and Mâcon. The decline of these rites came with the Gregorian reforms and the *Sacramentarium Hadrianum*, both of which contributed to the development of a uniform Roman Rite for the Carolingian Empire. This rite became the basis for the liturgy celebrated throughout Western Christianity.

Origins of the Lorrha Missal

The Lorrha Missal—or more precisely "Tallaght Recension"[4]—is a liturgical text from Ireland written in both Latin and Old Gaelic. It consists of sixty-seven folios of parchment, detailing the *ordo* for ordinary Mass, three votive masses, Baptism, and visitation of the sick. It also contains excerpts from the Gospel of John, three spells, and a Tract on the Mass.[5] The liturgical *ordines* contain numerous elements from both the Roman Rite and Gallican Rite, particularly from the Gelasian Sacramentary. Despite these influences, there

3. The term "Gallican Rite" is used within this book to reference the liturgical tradition of the Merovingian period. This is to remove the ambiguity that the term has accrued within liturgical studies. See Yitzhak Hen, "Liturgy of the Irish," 146.

4. As most scholars agree that the Lorrha Missal was originally composed in Tallaght, and since it was largely derived from the Romano-Gallican Gelasian Sacramentary with some localized adaptations, this designates it as a recension. For this reason, the "Tallaght Recension" serves as a more technically precise name. The name "Lorrha Missal" is used for the sake of relevancy. See John Ryan, "Sacraments," 374.

5. This tract is also recorded in the *Leabhar Breac*. See Meeder, "Destination and Function," 180.

are also unique aspects of the Missal that include an independently translated Constantinopolitan Creed[6] where *et filio* is used instead of *filioque.* The lack of distinction between the Proper and Ordinary and Canon of the Mass, and the placement of the Creed directly after the Gospel, have prompted scholars to argue for the existence of Byzantine or Eastern influences.[7]

Within the history of the Lorrha Missal, there have been several contributors that have provided additions or alterations over time. However, the earliest parts of the Missal were initially composed around the end of the 8th century. This has been determined by examining the litany of saints, where St. Máel Rúain was included within the main body of the text. As he was recorded to have died in 792 AD, the inclusion of his name at the end of the litany prompted scholars to determine that the Missal was most likely composed after St. Máel Rúain's death.[8] The Missal was later moved to the monastery in Lorrha in the 14th century, where the book-shrine (*cumhdach*) housing the text was constructed.

The purpose of the Missal has been debated by scholars, where early scholars such as Warner argued that it was meant to provide the Tallaght monastery with an authoritative ritual. Due to the inexpensive construction of the text, other scholars disagreed stating that it served as a *vade mecum* for itinerant priests. In more recent years, scholars such as O'Laughlin and Meeder have stated its use was within a monastic context but belonged to a monk-priest to serve a pastoral function. This position takes into the consideration that the presence of a deacon is necessary within the Order of Baptism, but that it was most likely intended for a small private audience.[9]

---

6. There are several deviations from the Gelasian Sacramentary, including but not limited to the phrases *et filio* and *unam sanctam aeclesiam catholicam et apostolicam.* See Breen, "Constantinopolitan Creed," 116—117.

7. See Breen, "Constantinopolitan Creed," 117.

8. See Nooij, "A New History," 93.

9. See Nooij, 89.

The Móel Cáich Alterations

A curious aspect of the Lorrha Missal are instances of alterations made by a scribe self-referenced as "Móel Cáich." A follower within an 8th century reform movement called *Céilí Dé*, he provided several alterations to the original text most likely to attract more people with hopes that they may 'return into the fold.'[10] This includes the addition of several rubrics in Old Gaelic, such as the "half-covering" (*lethdirech sund*) found after the litany and oblatory prayer.

The scribe added several prayers that reference the dawn (*exsultantes gaudio pro reddita nobis hums diei luce... resurgentem in hoc diluculo dominum dipraecamur... de lucub lucis auctore resurgente exultemus...*),[11] indicating that the Gospel reading took place at dawn where the Mass was celebrated in the open air. This contrasts with the original scribes who would've celebrated Mass in an enclosed oratory. He altered various prayers, including the *Hanc igitur* to which he extended significantly. He included prayers that indicate the use of incense, creating a more dramatic liturgy. Given that this was an expensive commodity in early medieval Ireland, the introduction of incense would entail the possibility that the scribe intended for a larger congregation.

While these changes point to someone more concerned with utility over tradition, the scribe also made alterations to suit his preferences. This includes the addition of the *filioque* clause, illustrating his interest in appealing towards the innovations within continental Europe. The scribe added various saints to the canon, particularly those originating from the middle region of Ireland. These alterations illustrate the religious and social environment, where it is observed that the scribe balanced between tradition, relevance within his local community, and the ongoings of the Western church.

10. See Hunwicke, "Revisited," 13.

11. This prayer is also present in the Antiphonary of Bangor, indicating a shared common liturgical heritage. See Hunwicke, "Revisited," 8.

Purpose of this Book

The *Aifreann na hÉireann* is a liturgical book that contains a recon-structed and original translation of the Lorrha Missal. Translated as "Irish Mass,"[12] this text contains material necessary for ordinary mass, three votive masses dedicated to penitents, martyrs, and the dead, baptism, and visitation of the sick. This includes a series of rubrics for ordinary Mass, based on the Tract of the Mass. Each service is written for the purpose of corporate worship, indicating what is said by the Priest, Deacon, or Reader in some circumstanc-es, and a response for the person or people in attendance. When it is not explicitly indicated, the responses are in bold.

Together with the *Portús na hÉireann*, these texts form a com-plete Gaelic Rite[13] inherited from the Gallican tradition and prac-ticed among early Irish monks.[14] As the *Portús* allows Christians to engage in solitary or corporate worship in a traditional manner, consistent with how Early Irish monks would pray the Daily Of-fice throughout the day, the *Aifreann* allows them to celebrate the death and resurrection of our LORD Jesus Christ. Celebrating the Mass contained therein provides the opportunity for Christians to connect with the spirituality and *ethos* of the Early Irish Church, participating in Christ as it was known to them.

---

12. The term *aifreann* is derived from the Latin *offerenda*, most likely adapted from the Ambrosian Rite as it is not present within any other liturgical tradition. See Ryan, "Sacraments," 373.

13. Given the presence of the Eucharistic antiphon *Hoc sacrum corpus* within the Antiphonary of Bangor and Lorrha Missal, and attribution of the *Navigatio* and Antiphonary to the Columbanian tradition, it can be argued that these texts share a common liturgical heritage albeit with changes and additions made over time. See Stevenson, "Monastic Rules of Columbanus," 211—212.

14. The term "Gaelic Rite" is preferred over "Celtic Rite" for the sake of accuracy, as we have little to no liturgical material from the ancient British church, making it impossible to ascertain any relationship regarding shared liturgical practice.

—

The Order of Mass

Introit

The litany of the apostles and martyrs of the confessors and virgins begins with the people standing

Priest: O God, make speed to save us.

People: **O LORD, make haste to help us.**

Priest: Glory be to the Father, and to the Son, and the Holy Spirit, as it was, as it is, as it shall be through the ages of ages. **Amen.**

Priest: We have sinned, O LORD, we have sinned, spare us our sins, and save us; You who guided Noah over the flood waves, hear us; who with your word recalled Jonah from the abyss, deliver us; who stretched forth your hand to Peter as he sank, help us, O Christ. Son of God, you accomplished marvelous things of the LORD with our fathers, be favorable in our days also; Stretch forth your hand from on high.

Priest: Deliver us, O Christ.

People: **Hear us, O Christ.**

Priest: Hear us, O Christ.

People: **Hear us, O LORD have mercy.**

Priest: Son of God, you who did marvelous things of the LORD with our fathers, be favorable in our days also; Stretch forth your hand from on high. Deliver us, O Christ.

People: **Hear us, O Christ.**

Saint Mary, **pray for us.**

Saint Peter, **pray for us.**

Saint Paul, **pray for us.**

Saint Andrew, **pray for us.**

Saint James, **pray for us.**

Saint Bartholomew, **pray for us.**

Saint Thomas, **pray for us.**

Saint Matthew, **pray for us.**

Saint James, **pray for us.**

Saint Madianus, **pray for us.**

Saint Mark, **pray for us.**

Saint Luke, **pray for us.**

All the Holy Saints, **pray for us.**

Prayer of St. Augustine

All our righteousnesses are unclean like a filthy rag. O Jesus Christ, we are unworthy that we may be living, but you who does not want the death of sinners; grant us forgiveness who are made of flesh so that through the labors of penance we may enjoy eternal life in heaven; through Christ our LORD who reigns with you and the Holy Spirit, now and ever, and unto the ages of ages. **Amen.**

Priest: May our prayer ascend to the throne of your glory, O LORD, and may our request not be returned to us in vain; we ask of this through our LORD Jesus Christ, who lives with you and the Holy Spirit, now and forever, and unto the ages of ages. **Amen.**

In the solemnity of Peter and Christ

O God, who to Blessed Peter, your Apostle the Pontiff, entrusted the keys of the heavenly kingdom, to bind and loosen souls, accept our prayers and through his intercession, O LORD, help us to be freed from the bondage of our sins; through our LORD Jesus Christ, who lives with you and the Holy Spirit, now and forever, and unto the ages of ages. **Amen.**

The Angelic Hymn

Gloria in Excelsis Deo

Glory to God in the highest,
and on earth peace to people of good will.
We praise you,
we bless you,
we adore you,
we glorify you,
we give you thanks for your great glory,
LORD God, heavenly King,
O God almighty Father.
LORD Jesus Christ, Only Begotten Son,
LORD God, Lamb of God, Son of The Father,
you take away the sins of the world,
have mercy on us;
you take away the sins of the world,
receive our prayer;
you are seated at the right hand of the Father
have mercy on us.
For you alone are the Holy One,
you alone are the LORD,
you alone are the Most High,
Jesus Christ,
with the Holy Spirit,
in the glory of God the Father.

Amen.

For those who turn from God and transgress daily

O God, who has prepared unattainable goods for those devoted to you, pour forth into our hearts the feeling of your love, so that we may follow you in all things, and above all things we may pursue your promises which surpasses all expectations; through Jesus Christ our LORD, who lives with you and the Holy Spirit, now and forever, and unto the ages of ages. **Amen.**

The First Prayer of Peter

O God, who is offended by the guilty and is appeased by penitence: Hear the groans of the afflicted; through Jesus Christ our LORD, who lives with you and the Holy Spirit, now and forever, and unto the ages of ages. **Amen.**

The Amplification

O God, who by ruling us, preserves us by sparing and justifying us: Deliver us from temporal tribulation and grant us eternal joys; through Jesus Christ our LORD, who lives with you and the Holy Spirit, now and forever, and unto the ages of ages. **Amen.**

Lesson Reading

The people sit. The appointed lesson is read by the Reader.

Here is the First Lesson.

Reader: The word of the LORD.

People: **Amen, thanks be to God.**

Priest: Almighty God for ever and ever, who redeemed your people from the works of the devil with the Blood of your Only-Begotten: Break the bonds of sin, so that those who are drawn to eternal life in the confession of your Name owe nothing to the author of death; through Jesus Christ our LORD, who lives with you and the Holy Spirit, now and forever, and unto the ages of ages. **Amen.**

The Gradual

Here is the Psalm; the last verse is treated as an antiphon. The people stand.

Priest: May the gifts by which the mysteries of our freedom and life are celebrated be pleasing to you, O LORD; through Jesus Christ our LORD, who lives with you and the Holy Spirit, now and forever, and unto the ages of ages. **Amen. Alleluia.**

The Sequence

Here is the Sequence.

Priest: O LORD, we ask that you be appeased by this sacrifice that our devotions may let us proceed to salvation; through Jesus Christ our LORD, who lives with you and the Holy Spirit, now and forever, and unto the ages of ages. **Amen.**

The Litany of St. Martin

Priest: Let us all say, "O LORD, hear us and have mercy upon us. O LORD, have mercy" with all our heart and mind.

Priest: With all our heart and with all our mind, to you who looks upon the earth and makes it tremble, let us pray:

People: **O LORD, hear us and have mercy upon us. O LORD, have mercy.**

Priest: For the most profound peace and tranquility of our times; for the holy catholic Church, which is from one end of the earth to the other, let us pray:

People: **O LORD, hear us and have mercy upon us. O LORD, have mercy.**

Priest: For the Pastor and Bishop N., and for all the bishops, priests, deacons, and all the clergy, let us pray:

People: **O LORD, hear us and have mercy upon us. O LORD, have mercy.**

Priest: For this place and those who dwell in it, for the world's leaders and all the nations' armies, let us pray:

People: **O LORD, hear us and have mercy upon us. O LORD, have mercy.**

Priest: For all those who have been ordained in exaltation for virgins, widows and orphans, let us pray:

People: **O LORD, hear us and have mercy upon us. O LORD, have mercy.**

Priest: For pilgrims and travelers by land, water, air, and space, penitents, and catechumens, let us pray:

People: **O LORD, hear us and have mercy upon us. O LORD, have mercy.**

Priest: For these who in the holy Church give the fruits of mercy, O LORD God of virtue, hear our prayers, we pray:

People: **O LORD, hear us and have mercy upon us. O LORD, have mercy.**

Priest: Let us be mindful of the Saints, Apostles and Martyrs, that by their prayers for us we may receive forgiveness, we pray:

People: **O LORD, hear us and have mercy upon us. O LORD, have mercy.**

Priest: We beseech the LORD to grant us a Christian and peaceful end:

People: **Grant it, O LORD, grant it.**

Priest: We beseech the LORD that the holy bond of Charity may continue in us:

People: **Grant it, O LORD, grant it.**

Priest: We beseech the LORD to preserve the sanctity and the purity of the catholic faith:

People: **Grant it, O LORD, grant it.**

Priest: Let us pray:

People: **O LORD have mercy.**

The Collect after the Litany

O LORD, graciously attend the celebration of this sacrifice to you, which may cleanse us from the sins of our condition and restore us to acceptability in your Name, through Jesus Christ our LORD, who lives with you and the Holy Spirit, now and forever, and unto the ages of ages. **Amen.**

Another

Before your eyes, O LORD, I stand while accused by the witness of a guilty conscience. I do not ask for others that I do not deserve to obtain. O LORD, forgive those who confess, those who sin, those who call upon you for forgiveness, for in your sacrament my perception is infirmed. Grant O LORD, you who does not receive our words with a hard heart that, through you, may mercy be granted;

through Jesus Christ our LORD, who lives with you and the Holy Spirit, now and forever, and unto the ages of ages. **Amen.**

Priest: Let my prayer be set forth in your sight as incense and let the lifting up of my hands be as an evening sacrifice. *Sung three times.*

Priest: Come, O LORD, the almighty sanctifier, and bless this sacrifice prepared for you. *Sung three times.*

The Prayer of St. Gregory

We beseech you, O LORD Almighty God, to graciously look upon our prayers offered to you and extend the right hand of your majesty to our defense; through Jesus Christ our LORD, who lives with you and the Holy Spirit, now and forever, and unto the ages of ages. **Amen.**

Gospel Lesson

Priest: The Gospel of our LORD according to Saint N.

People: **Glory be to you, O LORD.**

Here is the Gospel reading.

Priest: Pray for us and lift up the Gospel towards us.

The Sermon

The Sermon is given here. The people sit.

Symbol of Faith

Priest and People: **We believe in one God, the Father Almighty, maker of heaven and earth, of all things seen and unseen; we**

believe in one LORD Jesus Christ, the only-begotten Son of God, born from the Father before all ages, light from light, true God from true God, begotten, not made, of one being with the Father, through whom all things were made; who for us and for our salvation He came down from heaven, and was incarnate by the Holy Spirit of the Virgin Mary, and became man; and was crucified for us under Pontius Pilate; he suffered and was buried; and on the third day he rose again, according to the Scriptures; and ascended into heaven, and sits at the right hand of the Father; He will come again with glory to judge the living and the dead; of whose kingdom there will be no end; We believe in the Holy Spirit, the Lord and giver of life, who proceeds from the Father, who with the Father and the Son is worshipped and glorified, who has spoken through the prophets; we believe in one holy Church, catholic and apostolic. We confess one baptism for the remission of sins; we look for the resurrection of the dead and the life of the world to come. Amen.

Priest: O LORD, show us your mercy and grant us your salvation. *Sung three times.*

The Elevation

Priest: O LORD, sanctify the gifts offered to you and cleanse us from the stains of our sins; through Jesus Christ our LORD, who lives with you and the Holy Spirit, now and forever, and unto the ages of ages. **Amen.**

O LORD, we beseech you to accept these offerings of our devotion, and through the glorious sacrifice of your subjects purify our hearts; through Jesus Christ our LORD, who lives with you and the Holy Spirit, now and forever, and unto the ages of ages. **Amen.**

May these offerings of your people be acceptable to you, O LORD, which we offer in honor of our LORD Jesus Christ, who suffered for us and on the third day rose from the dead; for the souls of our loved ones N. and N.; of our dear ones whose names we recite; and whose names we do not recite but are recited by you in the Book of Eternal Life; of your mercy, rescue them who reigns now and forever, and unto the ages of ages. **Amen.**

Collect of the Preface

May this offering of your people be pleasing to you, which we offer to you in honor of our LORD Jesus Christ; and in commemoration of your blessed Apostles, and your Martyrs and Confessors, of whom we specially remember N., and for those whose feast is celebrated today; for the souls of all our Bishops, Priests, and Deacons, our children, and our penitents; may all proceed to salvation through Jesus Christ our LORD, who lives with you and the Holy Spirit, now and forever, and unto the ages of ages. **Amen.**

Holy Communion

Priest: Lift up your hearts.

People: **We lift them up to the LORD.**

Priest: Let us give thanks to the LORD our God.

People: **It is meet and right.**

Priest: It is truly meet and right, that we here always and everywhere give thanks to you, through Christ our LORD, to you, holy LORD Almighty and everlasting God; who with your Only-Begotten and the Holy Spirit, O God, are One and Immortal God; Incorruptible and Immovable God; Unseen and Faithful God; Wonderful and Praiseworthy God; Honorable and Mighty God; Most High and Magnificent God; Living and True God; Wise and Powerful God; Correct and Beautiful God; Great and Good God; Terrible and Peaceful God; Noble and Upright God; Pure and Kind God; Blessed and Just God; Righteous and Holy God, not in the singleness of person but Trinity of one substance. We believe in you, we bless you, we worship you, and praise your Name forever and ever; through whom the Salvation of the World; through whom is the life of man; through whom is the resurrection of the dead.

Through whom the Angels praise your Majesty, the Dominions adore you, the Powers of Heaven tremble, and the Virtues and the blessed Seraphim unite in triumphant chorus to celebrate your Majesty. With whom we entreat you to bid our voices to be admitted as we acclaim:

Sanctus

Choir and People: **Holy, Holy, Holy, LORD God of Sabaoth. Heaven and the whole earth are full of your glory, Hosanna in the highest. Blessed is he who came in the Name of the LORD; Hosanna in the highest.**

Priest: Blessed is He who came from heaven that He might dwell on earth, was made man to destroy the sins of the flesh, became a sacrifice through His passion to give eternal life to those that believe; through Jesus Christ our LORD, who lives with you and the Holy Spirit, now and forever, and unto the ages of ages. **Amen.**

Canon of Pope Gelasius

Priest: Therefore, most merciful Father, through Jesus Christ your son our LORD: We beseech you, and we ask you to accept and bless these gifts, these offerings, these holy sacrifices, which first of all we offer to you for your holy catholic Church; that you may keep her in peace, to guard, unify, and govern her throughout the whole world together with to your most blessed servants, our Patriarchs, Bishops, and to all orthodox and apostolic worshipers of the faith, and to our Metropolitan N. and Bishop N.; remember also, O LORD, your servants and maidens N. and N., (*Names of the living are recited here*) and all those present here, whose faith and devotion is known to you, who offer you this sacrifice of praise, for themselves and for all of theirs; for the redemption of their souls; for their body of elders and of all his ministers; for the integrity of virgins and the continence of widows; for the temperature of the air; and the fruitfulness of the earth; for the return of peace and an end to conflicts; for the safety of our leaders and the peace of the people; and the return of captives and for the prayers of those present today; for the commemoration of martyrs; for the forgiveness of our sins and the correction of their deeds; for the repose of the dead; and the purity of our journey; for the Patriarch, Bishop and all the Bishops, Priests, and all in Holy Orders; for all Christian leaders; for our brothers and sisters; for our brethren who follow the right way; for our brethren whom the LORD has deigned to bring out of the murky darkness of this world, may divine mercy receive them in the eternal rest of the highest light; for our brethren who are afflicted with various sorrows, may the divine mercy take care of them for the hope of their salvation and integrity.

The Nativity of the Lord

And celebrating this most holy day, on which pure virginity brought forth the Savior into this world;

The Feast of the Circumcision

And celebrating the most holy day of the circumcision of our LORD Jesus Christ;

Epiphany

And celebrating the most holy day of the Supper of our LORD Jesus Christ;

Easter

And the most holy night *or* day of the Resurrection of our LORD Jesus Christ;

The Closing of Easter

And celebrating the most holy day of the end of the Passover of our LORD Jesus Christ;

Ascension

And celebrating the most holy day of the Ascension of our LORD Jesus Christ;

Pentecost

And celebrating the most holy day of the Pentecost of our LORD Jesus Christ on which the Holy Spirit descended upon the Apostles;

Priest: And venerating the memory, first of all, of the glorious Ever-Virgin Mary, the Mother of God and our LORD Jesus Christ, and to your blessed Apostles and martyrs: Peter and Paul, Andrew, James, John, Thomas, James, Philip, Bartholomew, Matthew, Simon and Thaddeus, Anne, Clement, Cornelius, Cyprian, Laurence, Chrysoginus, John, Paul, Cosmas, and Damian, and of all your Saints by whose merits and prayers that you may grant us, that we may be strengthened with the help of your protection in all things; through Jesus Christ our LORD, who lives with you and the Holy Spirit, now and forever, and unto the ages of ages. **Amen.**

Priest: Therefore we offer this oblation of our servitude and of your whole family, which we offer to you in honor of our LORD Jesus Christ, and in commemoration of your blessed martyrs in this church, which your servants built in honor of your glorious Name;

through Jesus Christ our LORD, who lives with you and the Holy Spirit, now and forever, and unto the ages of ages. **Amen.**

Priest: Order our days in your peace, deliver us from eternal damnation, and number us among your Elect; through Jesus Christ our LORD, who lives with you and the Holy Spirit, now and forever, and unto the ages of ages. **Amen.**

Priest: Which offering to you, O God, we beseech you to be pleased in all things to make blessed, ratified, reasonable and acceptable, and to make us worthy to become the Body and Blood of your most beloved Son, our LORD Jesus Christ, who on the day before he suffered, took bread into His holy and venerable hands, He gave thanks to you, he blessed, broke it, and gave it to his disciples, saying, "Take and eat from this, all of you, for this is my Body." In the same way after He had eaten, He took this excellent cup into his holy and venerable hands. Also, giving thanks to you, He blessed it and gave it to his disciples, saying, "Take and drink from this, all of you, for this is the holy chalice of my Blood, of the new and eternal testament, the mystery of faith, which is shed for you and for many in the remission of sins. Whenever you do these things in memory of me, you will preach my passion, announce my resurrection, and hope for my coming until I come to you again from heaven."

Priest: Wherefore, O LORD, we your servants, together with your holy people, remember the blessed passion and death of Christ your Son our LORD, of his resurrection from hell and glorious ascension into heaven: We offer unto your excellent majesty of your own gifts and bounty, to accept them as you have deigned to receive the gifts of your righteous son Abel, and the sacrifice of our patriarch Abraham, and the Holy Sacrifice, the Spotless Host, that your high priest Melchizedek offered to you. We beseech and pray to you, Almighty God to command these things to be carried out by the hands of your holy angel to your sublime altar, in the presence of your divine Majesty, that as many of us as we have taken from this altar of sanctification the sacred Body and Blood of your Most Holy Son, may be filled with all blessings and grace.

Priest: Remember also, O LORD, those who have gone before us with the sign of faith and rest in the peace of Christ, N. With all throughout the whole world who offer the spiritual sacrifices to God the Father, and the Son, and the Holy Spirit, our senior, the Priest N. with the holy and venerable Priests, offers for himself, for his own, and for the whole assembly of the catholic Church; and in commemoration of the wrestling of the venerable Patriarchs, Prophets, Apostles, Martyrs, and of all the Saints, that they may deign to intercede for us before the LORD our God:

Saint Stephen, **pray for us.**

Saint Martin, **pray for us.**

Saint Jerome, **pray for us.**

Saint Augustine, **pray for us.**

Saint Gregory, **pray for us.**

Saint Hilary, **pray for us.**

Saint Patrick, **pray for us.**

Saint Ailbe, **pray for us.**

Saint Finnian, **pray for us.**

Saint Finnian, **pray for us.**

Saint Ciaran, **pray for us.**

Saint Ciaran, **pray for us.**

Saint Brendan, **pray for us.**

Saint Brendan, **pray for us.**

Saint Columba, **pray for us.**

Saint Columba, **pray for us.**

Saint Comgall, **pray for us.**

Saint Cainnech, **pray for us.**

Saint Finbar, **pray for us.**

Saint Nessan, **pray for us.**

Saint Fachtna, **pray for us.**

Saint Lua, **pray for us.**

Saint Lacten, **pray for us.**

Saint Ruadhan, pray for us.

Saint Carthage, **pray for us.**

Saint Kevin, **pray for us.**

Saint Mochoemog, **pray for us.**

Saint Brigid, **pray for us.**

Saint Ite, **pray for us.**

Saint Scetha, **pray for us.**

Saint Sinecha, **pray for us.**

Saint Samthann, **pray for us.**

Priest: All you Saints,

People: **pray for us.**

Priest: Be propitious to us, O LORD, spare us.

People: **Be propitious to us, O LORD, deliver us from all evil.**

Priest: Deliver us, O LORD, through your cross.

People: **Deliver us, O LORD, we beg you, hear us, O Son.**

Priest: We beg you, hear us, that you may grant peace.

People: **We beg you, hear us, Lamb of God, who takes away the sins of the world, have mercy on us.**

Priest: Christ, hear us.

People: **Christ, hear us.**

Priest: Christ, hear us.

Prayer of St. Ambrose

Priest: Before the sight of your divine majesty, O God, I stand daring to invoke your holy Name. Have mercy on me, O LORD, a sinful man, clinging to the impure mud. Forgive this unworthy Priest through whose hands this offering seems to be presented. Spare me, O LORD, tainted by the stain of sins, especially those of a grave nature, and do not enter into judgment with your servant, for no one living is justified in your sight. Burdened by the desires and wills of the flesh, we beseech you, O LORD, to remember that we are mere flesh and there is no other to be compared to you in your sight. For these, your servants: *Here the Priest commemorates the names of the deceased.*

Priest: We entreat you to grant them indulgence in light and peace.

Priest: To us sinners also, your servants, who hope for the multitude of your mercies, deign to grant some part and fellowship with your Holy Apostles and Martyrs: with Peter, Paul, Patrick; John, Stephen, Matthias, Barnabas, Ignatius, Alexander, Marcellinus, Peter, Perpetua, Agnes, Cecilia, Felicity, Anastasia, Agatha, Lucia, and with all your Saints; within whose fellowship we beseech you to admit us, not considering our merit but granting us forgiveness, through Jesus Christ our LORD, through whom, O LORD, +create, +sanctify, +renew, +bless, and bestow all these good things upon us. Through +Him, and with +Him, and in +Him, in the unity of the Holy Spirit, all honor and glory is yours, God the Father Almighty, now and ever, and unto the Ages of ages. **Amen.**

Priest: Let your mercy be upon us, O LORD, as we have hoped in you.

Choir and People: **They have known the LORD, alleluia,**
in the breaking of the bread, alleluia.
The bread which we break is the Body of our LORD Jesus Christ, alleluia.
The cup that we bless, alleluia,
is the Blood of our LORD Jesus Christ, alleluia,
for the remission of our sins. Alleluia.
May your mercy, O LORD, be upon us, alleluia,
as we have hoped in you, alleluia.
They have known the LORD, alleluia.

Priest: We believe, O LORD. We believe that we are redeemed in this breaking of the Body and pouring forth of the Blood; we shall rely on the reception of this Sacrament for our fortification, we may enjoy in the true fruits of heaven; through Jesus Christ our LORD, who lives with you and the Holy Spirit, now and forever, and unto the ages of ages. **Amen.**

Divine Prayer

Priest: Having been taught by divine instruction and shaped by divine institution, we dare to say:

People: **Our Father in heaven, hallowed be your Name; your kingdom come, your will be done, on earth as it is in heaven. Give us today our substantial bread. Forgive us our debts as we**

forgive our debtors. Keep us from falling into temptation and deliver us from evil.

Priest: For yours is the kingdom, and the power, and the glory of the Father, and the Son, and Holy Spirit, now and ever, and unto the ages of ages. **Amen.**

Priest: Deliver us, O LORD, from every evil, past, present, and future, and through the intercessions of your blessed Apostles Peter, Paul, and Patrick, grant us your gracious peace in our days, that assisted by the aid of your mercy we may always be free from sin and secure from every distress; through Jesus Christ our LORD, who lives with you and the Holy Spirit, now and forever, and unto the ages of ages. **Amen.**

The Offering of Peace

Priest: May the peace and love of our LORD Jesus Christ, and the Communion of all the Saints be with us always.

People: **And with your spirit.**

Priest: You commanded peace, you gave us peace, you left us peace: O LORD, grant us your peace from heaven and may you make this day and the rest of the days of our life peaceful; through Jesus Christ our LORD, who lives with you and the Holy Spirit, now and forever, and unto the ages of ages. **Amen.**

Priest: May the mixing of the Body and Blood of our LORD Jesus Christ be for us salvation unto eternal life. **Amen.**

The Confraction

While the litany is sung, the Priest recites Psalms 22, 23, 24, and 42 in a low voice.

Priest: Behold the Lamb of God; behold him who takes away the sins of the world.

Choir and People: **My peace I give to you, alleluia.**

My peace I leave with you, alleluia.

Abundant peace is for those who are attentive to your law, O LORD, alleluia,

and there is no stumbling for them, alleluia.

For the King of Heaven with peace, alleluia.

Who is full of the promise of life, alleluia.

Sing to him a new song, alleluia.

All you Saints come forth, alleluia.

Come, eat my bread, alleluia,

and drink the wine which had been mixed for you, alleluia.

Whoever eats my body and drinks my blood, alleluia,

Shall abide in me, and I in him, alleluia.

This is the Bread of Life that came down from heaven, alleluia,

whoever eats from it will live forever. Alleluia.

The LORD gave them the bread of heaven. Alleluia,

Man ate the bread of angels. Alleluia.

Eat, my friends, alleluia,

and be intoxicated, my beloved, alleluia.

Take this sacred body and blood of the LORD and Savior, alleluia,

for yourselves unto eternal life, alleluia.

Upon my lips, I will meditate on a hymn, alleluia,

which you taught me, alleluia,

and I will respond with righteousness, alleluia.

I shall bless the LORD at all times, alleluia.

His praise shall always be in my mouth, alleluia.

Taste and see, alleluia,

how sweet the LORD is, alleluia.

Where I shall be, alleluia,

there also will be my minister, alleluia.

Allow the little ones to come to me, alleluia,

and do not hinder them, alleluia.

For of such is the kingdom of heaven, alleluia.

Devote yourselves to penitence, alleluia,

for the kingdom of heaven is at hand, alleluia.

The kingdom of heaven suffers violence, alleluia.

And the violent take it by force, alleluia.

Come forth and take possession of the kingdom of my Father, alleluia.

Which has been prepared for you since the beginning of the world, alleluia.

Priest: Grant, O LORD, that those whom you have satisfied with heavenly gifts, may be cleansed from their hidden sins and we may be set free from the snares of the enemy. **Amen.**

Postcommunion Prayer

We give thanks to you, O LORD, Holy Father, Almighty and eternal God, who has satisfied us by the Communion of the Body and Blood of Christ your Son: We humbly implore for your mercy, that this your Sacrament may not bring condemnation unto punishment, but may be an intercession for salvation, a remission of sins, a strengthening for the weak, a defense against the dangers of the world; may this Communion purify us from our faults and grant us to be participants in heavenly joy; through Jesus Christ our LORD, who lives with you and the Holy Spirit, now and forever, and unto the ages of ages. **Amen.**

The Dismissal

Priest: The Mass has been celebrated in peace.

People: **Amen, thanks be to God.**

The Order of Mass for Apostles and Holy Martyrs

Introit

The litany of the apostles and martyrs of the confessors and virgins begins with the people standing

Priest: O God, make speed to save us.

People: **O LORD, make haste to help us.**

Priest: Glory be to the Father, and to the Son, and the Holy Spirit, as it was, as it is, as it shall be through the ages of ages. **Amen.**

Priest: We have sinned, O LORD, we have sinned, spare us our sins, and save us; You who guided Noah over the flood waves, hear us; who with your word recalled Jonah from the abyss, deliver us; who stretched forth your hand to Peter as he sank, help us, O Christ. Son of God, you accomplished marvelous things of the LORD with our fathers, be favorable in our days also; Stretch forth your hand from on high.

Priest: Deliver us, O Christ.

People: **Hear us, O Christ.**

Priest: Hear us, O Christ.

People: **Hear us, O LORD have mercy.**

Priest: Son of God, you who did marvelous things of the LORD with our fathers, be favorable in our days also; Stretch forth your hand from on high. Deliver us, O Christ.

People: **Hear us, O Christ.**

Saint Mary, **pray for us.**

Saint Peter, **pray for us.**

Saint Paul, **pray for us.**

Saint Andrew, **pray for us.**

Saint James, **pray for us.**

Saint Bartholomew, **pray for us.**

Saint Thomas, **pray for us.**

Saint Matthew, **pray for us.**

Saint James, **pray for us.**

Saint Madianus, **pray for us.**

Saint Mark, **pray for us.**

Saint Luke, **pray for us.**

All the Holy Saints, **pray for us.**

Prayer of St. Augustine

All our righteousnesses are unclean like a filthy rag. O Jesus Christ, we are unworthy that we may be living, but you who does not want the death of sinners; grant us forgiveness who are made of flesh so that through the labors of penance we may enjoy eternal life in heaven; through Christ our LORD who reigns with you and the Holy Spirit, now and ever, and unto the ages of ages. **Amen.**

Priest: May our prayer ascend to the throne of your glory, O LORD, and may our request not be returned to us in vain; we ask of this through our LORD Jesus Christ, who lives with you and the Holy Spirit, now and forever, and unto the ages of ages. **Amen.**

Priest: O God the Father, God the Son, and God the Holy Spirit, one and only Lord of Lords, and King of Kings, and the glory of things to come: We faithfully beseech you by the illustrious judgments of the Patriarchs; the glorious prophecies of the Prophets; the holy merits of the Apostles; the sufferings of the Martyrs; the faith of the Confessors; the sanctity of the Virgins; the contemplative life of the Anchorites; the spiritual silence of monks; the continuous prayers of all Holy Catholic and Apostolic Bishops, Abbots, and faithful leaders of all nations; and especially by the Holy Saints and Virgins whose solemnity we celebrate today, that this offering of your people, which we present to the Holy Trinity in honor of N., may be acceptable to God and may benefit all unto salvation; through Jesus Christ our LORD, who lives with you and the Holy Spirit, now and forever, and unto the ages of ages. **Amen.**

The Angelic Hymn

Gloria in Excelsis Deo

Glory to God in the highest,
and on earth peace to people of good will.
We praise you,
we bless you,
we adore you,
we glorify you,
we give you thanks for your great glory,
LORD God, heavenly King,
O God almighty Father.
LORD Jesus Christ, Only Begotten Son,
LORD God, Lamb of God, Son of The Father,
you take away the sins of the world,
have mercy on us;
you take away the sins of the world,
receive our prayer;

you are seated at the right hand of the Father
have mercy on us.
For you alone are the Holy One,
you alone are the LORD,
you alone are the Most High,
Jesus Christ,
with the Holy Spirit,
in the glory of God the Father.
Amen.

Priest: We give thanks to O LORD our God Jesus Christ, splendor of the Father's glory, and day of eternal brightness, for you deigned to illuminate your twelve Apostles with the fire of your Holy Spirit, as if they were the twelve hours of the day. For you said that "If, therefore, anyone walks in the light of day, he will not stumble." Shine upon us, O LORD our God, Jesus Christ, the Sun of Righteousness, in whose wings is healing for those who fear you, so that we may walk in the light while we have light, to be the sons of light. You illuminated the Apostles as lights for this world, and other Saints as your representatives, freely by the Holy Spirit and the foretold doctrine; dispel from us the darkness of ignorance, and through the patronage of these whose festival is celebrated today, eliminate the darkness of our righteousness, so that in you and through you, we may always abide; through Jesus Christ our LORD, who lives with you and the Holy Spirit, now and forever, and unto the ages of ages. **Amen.**

The First Prayer of Peter

O God, who is offended by the guilty and is appeased by penitence: Hear the groans of the afflicted; through Jesus Christ our LORD, who lives with you and the Holy Spirit, now and forever, and unto the ages of ages. **Amen.**

The Amplification

O God, who by ruling us, preserves us by sparing and justifying us: Deliver us from temporal tribulation and grant us eternal joys; through Jesus Christ our LORD, who lives with you and the Holy Spirit, now and forever, and unto the ages of ages. **Amen.**

Lesson Reading

The people sit. The appointed lesson is read by the Reader.

Here is the First Lesson.

Reader: The word of the LORD.

People: **Amen, thanks be to God.**

Priest: Almighty God for ever and ever, who redeemed your people from the works of the devil with the Blood of your Only-Begotten: Break the bonds of sin, so that those who are drawn to eternal life in the confession of your Name owe nothing to the author of death; through Jesus Christ our LORD, who lives with you and the Holy Spirit, now and forever, and unto the ages of ages. **Amen.**

The Gradual

Here is the Psalm; the last verse is treated as an antiphon. The people stand.

Priest: May the gifts by which the mysteries of our freedom and life are celebrated be pleasing to you, O LORD; through Jesus Christ our LORD, who lives with you and the Holy Spirit, now and forever, and unto the ages of ages. **Amen. Alleluia.**

The Sequence

Here is the Sequence.

Priest: O LORD, we ask that you be appeased by this sacrifice that our devotions may let us proceed to salvation; through Jesus Christ our LORD, who lives with you and the Holy Spirit, now and forever, and unto the ages of ages. **Amen.**

The Litany of St. Martin

Priest: Let us all say, "O LORD, hear us and have mercy upon us. O LORD, have mercy" with all our heart and mind.

Priest: With all our heart and with all our mind, to you who looks upon the earth and makes it tremble, let us pray:

People: **O LORD, hear us and have mercy upon us. O LORD, have mercy.**

Priest: For the most profound peace and tranquility of our times; for the holy catholic Church, which is from one end of the earth to the other, let us pray:

People: **O LORD, hear us and have mercy upon us. O LORD, have mercy.**

Priest: For the Pastor and Bishop N., and for all the bishops, priests, deacons, and all the clergy, let us pray:

People: **O LORD, hear us and have mercy upon us. O LORD, have mercy.**

Priest: For this place and those who dwell in it, for the world's leaders and all the nations' armies, let us pray:

People: **O LORD, hear us and have mercy upon us. O LORD, have mercy.**

Priest: For all those who have been ordained in exaltation for virgins, widows and orphans, let us pray:

People: **O LORD, hear us and have mercy upon us. O LORD, have mercy.**

Priest: For pilgrims and travelers by land, water, air, and space, penitents, and catechumens, let us pray:

People: **O LORD, hear us and have mercy upon us. O LORD, have mercy.**

Priest: For these who in the holy Church give the fruits of mercy, O LORD God of virtue, hear our prayers, we pray:

People: **O LORD, hear us and have mercy upon us. O LORD, have mercy.**

Priest: Let us be mindful of the Saints, Apostles and Martyrs, that by their prayers for us we may receive forgiveness, we pray:

People: **O LORD, hear us and have mercy upon us. O LORD, have mercy.**

Priest: We beseech the LORD to grant us a Christian and peaceful end:

People: **Grant it, O LORD, grant it.**

Priest: We beseech the LORD that the holy bond of Charity may continue in us:

People: **Grant it, O LORD, grant it.**

Priest: We beseech the LORD to preserve the sanctity and the purity of the catholic faith:

People: **Grant it, O LORD, grant it.**

Priest: Let us pray:

People: **O LORD have mercy.**

The Collect after the Litany

O LORD, graciously attend the celebration of this sacrifice to you, which may cleanse us from the sins of our condition and restore us to acceptability in your Name, through Jesus Christ our LORD, who lives with you and the Holy Spirit, now and forever, and unto the ages of ages. **Amen.**

Another

Before your eyes, O LORD, I stand while accused by the witness of a guilty conscience. I do not ask for others that I do not deserve to obtain. O LORD, forgive those who confess, those who sin, those who call upon you for forgiveness, for in your sacrament my perception is infirmed. Grant O LORD, you who does not receive our words with a hard heart that, through you, may mercy be granted; through Jesus Christ our LORD, who lives with you and the Holy Spirit, now and forever, and unto the ages of ages. **Amen.**

Priest: Let my prayer be set forth in your sight as incense and let the lifting up of my hands be as an evening sacrifice. *Sung three times.*

Priest: Come, O LORD, the almighty sanctifier, and bless this sacrifice prepared for you. *Sung three times.*

The Prayer of St. Gregory

We beseech you, O LORD Almighty God, to graciously look upon our prayers offered to you and extend the right hand of your majesty to our defense; through Jesus Christ our LORD, who lives with you and the Holy Spirit, now and forever, and unto the ages of ages. **Amen.**

Gospel Lesson

Priest: The Gospel of our LORD according to Saint N.

People: **Glory be to you, O LORD.**

Here is the Gospel reading.

Priest: Pray for us and lift up the Gospel towards us.

The Sermon

The Sermon is given here. The people sit.

Symbol of Faith

Priest and People: **We believe in one God, the Father Almighty, maker of heaven and earth, of all things seen and unseen; we believe in one LORD Jesus Christ, the only-begotten Son of God, born from the Father before all ages, light from light, true God from true God, begotten, not made, of one being with the Father, through whom all things were made; who for us and for our salvation He came down from heaven, and was incarnate by the Holy Spirit of the Virgin Mary, and became man; and was crucified for us under Pontius Pilate; he suffered and was buried; and on the third day he rose again, according to the Scriptures; and ascended into heaven, and sits at the right hand of the Father; He will come again with glory to judge the living and the dead; of whose kingdom there will be no end; We believe in the Holy Spirit, the Lord and giver of life, who proceeds from the Father, who with the Father and the Son is worshipped and glorified, who has spoken through the prophets; we believe in one holy Church, catholic and apostolic. We confess one baptism for the remission of sins; we look for the resurrection of the dead and the life of the world to come. Amen.**

Priest: O LORD, show us your mercy and grant us your salvation. *Sung three times.*

The Elevation

Priest: O LORD, sanctify the gifts offered to you and cleanse us from the stains of our sins; through Jesus Christ our LORD, who lives with you and the Holy Spirit, now and forever, and unto the ages of ages. **Amen.**

O LORD, we beseech you to accept these offerings of our devotion, and through the glorious sacrifice of your subjects purify our hearts; through Jesus Christ our LORD, who lives with you and the Holy Spirit, now and forever, and unto the ages of ages. **Amen.**

May these offerings of your people be acceptable to you, O LORD, which we offer in honor of our LORD Jesus Christ, who suffered for us and on the third day rose from the dead; for the souls of our loved ones N. and N.; of our dear ones whose names we recite; and whose names we do not recite but are recited by you in the Book of Eternal Life; of your mercy, rescue them who reigns now and forever, and unto the ages of ages. **Amen.**

Collect of the Preface

Priest: O God, who surrounds and protects us by the intercessions of your Holy and most blessed spirits of Angels, Archangels, Principalities, Powers, Dominions, Virtues, Cherubim, and Seraphim, Patriarchs, Prophets, Apostles, Martyrs, Confessors and Virgins, Hermits, and all the heavenly host of Saints: We beseech you to grant that we may make progress by their example, and by their intercession may we be defended from all perils; through Jesus Christ our LORD, who lives with you and the Holy Spirit, now and forever, and unto the ages of ages. **Amen.**

Holy Communion

Priest: Lift up your hearts.

People: **We lift them up to the LORD.**

Priest: Let us give thanks to the LORD our God.

People: **It is meet and right.**

Priest: It is truly meet and right, fitting and proper, glorious and praiseworthy that we should always give thanks to You, O LORD God Almighty, but on this day we owe you abundant gratitude with joyful spirits on the solemnity of the Apostles (or Saints) N. Therefore, grant us, Almighty God, faith, hope, and charity, a catholic faith, and peace through the example and commemoration of your Saints N., in whose honor this offering is presented today, that it may benefit all for salvation through our LORD Jesus Christ, to whom all angels and archangels, Prophets and Apostles, Martyrs and Confessors, Virgins and all Saints, with perpetual and untiring praise, together with the four beasts and the twenty-four elders, singing:

Another

Priest: O LORD Almighty God, who tests your Saints with measure and glorify them without measure, whose commandments have an aim but whose rewards have no end: Hear our prayers through the examples and tribulations of the martyrs; Grant us their patronage to assist us in the progress of faith, the fruit of good works, the blessings of prosperity, the advantages of well-being, the cultivation of piety, and the increase of divine fear. May the holy Martyrs pray for us, for our deceased, for our flocks and all the fruits of our land, and for all those dwelling in this place. To you, Almighty God, the creator of countless heavenly and earthly creatures, of your Saints, and the choirs of angels proclaim with unceasing voice, saying:

Sanctus

Choir and people: **Holy, Holy, Holy, LORD God of Sabaoth. Heaven and the whole earth are full of your glory, Hosanna in the highest. Blessed is he who came in the Name of the LORD; Hosanna in the highest.**

Priest: Blessed is He who came from heaven that He might dwell on earth, was made man to destroy the sins of the flesh, became a sacrifice through His passion to give eternal life to those that believe; through Jesus Christ our LORD, who lives with you and the Holy Spirit, now and forever, and unto the ages of ages. **Amen.**

Canon of Pope Gelasius

Priest: Therefore, most merciful Father, through Jesus Christ your son our LORD: We beseech you, and we ask you to accept and bless these gifts, these offerings, these holy sacrifices, which first of all we offer to you for your holy catholic Church; that you may keep her in peace, to guard, unify, and govern her throughout the whole world together with to your most blessed servants, our Patriarchs, Bishops, and to all orthodox and apostolic worshipers of the faith, and to our Metropolitan N. and Bishop N.; remember also, O LORD, your servants and maidens N. and N., (*Names of the living are recited here*) and all those present here, whose faith and devotion is known to you, who offer you this sacrifice of praise, for themselves and for all of theirs; for the redemption of their souls; for their body of elders and of all his ministers; for the integrity of virgins and the continence of widows; for the temperature of the air; and the fruitfulness of the earth; for the return of peace and an end to conflicts; for the safety of our leaders and the peace of the people; and the return of captives and for the prayers of those present today; for the commemoration of martyrs; for the forgiveness of our sins and the correction of their deeds; for the repose of the dead; and the purity of our journey; for the Patriarch, Bishop and all the Bishops, Priests, and all in Holy Orders; for all Christian leaders; for our brothers and sisters; for our brethren who follow the right way; for our brethren whom the LORD has deigned to bring out of the murky darkness of this world, may divine mercy receive them in the eternal rest of the highest light; for our brethren who are afflicted with various sorrows, may the divine mercy take care of them for the hope of their salvation and integrity.

The Nativity of the Lord

And celebrating this most Holy day, on which pure virginity brought forth the Savior into this world;

The Feast of the Circumcision

And celebrating the most holy day of the circumcision of our LORD Jesus Christ;

Epiphany

And celebrating the most holy day of the Supper of our LORD Jesus Christ;

Easter

And the most holy night *or* day of the Resurrection of our LORD Jesus Christ;

The Closing of Easter

And celebrating the most holy day of the end of the Passover of our LORD Jesus Christ;

Ascension

And celebrating the most holy day of the Ascension of our LORD Jesus Christ;

Pentecost

And celebrating the most holy day of the Pentecost of our LORD Jesus Christ on which the Holy Spirit descended upon the Apostles;

Priest: And venerating the memory, first of all, of the glorious Ever-Virgin Mary, the Mother of God and our LORD Jesus Christ, and to your blessed Apostles and martyrs: Peter and Paul, Andrew, James, John, Thomas, James, Philip, Bartholomew, Matthew, Simon and Thaddeus, Anne, Clement, Cornelius, Cyprian, Laurence, Chrysoginus, John, Paul, Cosmas, and Damian, and of all your Saints by whose merits and prayers that you may grant us, that we may be strengthened with the help of your protection in all things; through Jesus Christ our LORD, who lives with you and the Holy Spirit, now and forever, and unto the ages of ages. **Amen.**

Priest: Therefore we offer this oblation of our servitude and of your whole family, which we offer to you in honor of our LORD Jesus Christ, and in commemoration of your blessed martyrs in this church, which your servants built in honor of your glorious Name; through Jesus Christ our LORD, who lives with you and the Holy Spirit, now and forever, and unto the ages of ages. **Amen.**

Priest: Order our days in your peace, deliver us from eternal damnation, and number us among your Elect; through Jesus Christ our LORD, who lives with you and the Holy Spirit, now and forever, and unto the ages of ages. **Amen.**

Priest: Which offering to you, O God, we beseech you to be pleased in all things to make blessed, ratified, reasonable and acceptable, and to make us worthy to become the Body and Blood of your most beloved Son, our LORD Jesus Christ, who on the day before he suffered, took bread into His holy and venerable hands, He gave thanks to you, he blessed, broke it, and gave it to his disciples, saying, "Take and eat from this, all of you, for this is my Body." In the same way after He had eaten, He took this excellent cup into his holy and venerable hands. Also, giving thanks to you, He blessed it and gave it to his disciples, saying, "Take and drink from this, all of you, for this is the holy chalice of my Blood, of the new and eternal testament, the mystery of faith, which is shed for you and for many in the remission of sins. Whenever you do these things in memory of me, you will preach my passion, announce my resurrection, and hope for my coming until I come to you again from heaven."

Priest: Wherefore, O LORD, we your servants, together with your holy people, remember the blessed passion and death of Christ your Son our LORD, of his resurrection from hell and glorious ascension into heaven: We offer unto your excellent majesty of your own gifts and bounty, to accept them as you have deigned to receive the gifts of your righteous son Abel, and the sacrifice of our patriarch Abraham, and the Holy Sacrifice, the Spotless Host, that your high priest Melchizedek offered to you. We beseech and pray to you, Almighty God to command these things to be carried out by the hands of your holy angel to your sublime altar, in the presence of your divine Majesty, that as many of us as we have taken from this altar of sanctification the sacred Body and Blood of your Most Holy Son, may be filled with all blessings and grace.

Priest: Remember also, O LORD, those who have gone before us with the sign of faith and rest in the peace of Christ, N. With all throughout the whole world who offer the spiritual sacrifices to God the Father, and the Son, and the Holy Spirit, our senior, the Priest N. with the holy and venerable Priests, offers for himself, for his own, and for the whole assembly of the catholic Church; and in commemoration of the wrestling of the venerable Patriarchs, Prophets, Apostles, Martyrs, and of all the Saints, that they may deign to intercede for us before the LORD our God:

Saint Stephen, **pray for us.**

Saint Martin, **pray for us.**

Saint Jerome, **pray for us.**

Saint Augustine, **pray for us.**

Saint Gregory, **pray for us.**

Saint Hilary, **pray for us.**

Saint Patrick, **pray for us.**

Saint Ailbe, **pray for us.**

Saint Finnian, **pray for us.**

Saint Finnian, **pray for us.**

Saint Ciaran, **pray for us.**

Saint Ciaran, **pray for us.**

Saint Brendan, **pray for us.**

Saint Brendan, **pray for us.**

Saint Columba, **pray for us.**

Saint Columba, **pray for us.**

Saint Comgall, **pray for us.**

Saint Cainnech, **pray for us.**

Saint Finbar, **pray for us.**

Saint Nessan, **pray for us.**

Saint Fachtna, **pray for us.**

Saint Lua, **pray for us.**

Saint Lacten, **pray for us.**

Saint Ruadhan, pray for us.

Saint Carthage, **pray for us.**

Saint Kevin, **pray for us.**

Saint Mochoemog, **pray for us.**

Saint Brigid, **pray for us.**

Saint Ite, **pray for us.**

Saint Scetha, **pray for us.**

Saint Sinecha, **pray for us.**

Saint Samthann, **pray for us.**

Priest: All you Saints,

People: **pray for us.**

Priest: Be propitious to us, O LORD, spare us.

People: **Be propitious to us, O LORD, deliver us from all evil.**

Priest: Deliver us, O LORD, through your cross.

People: **Deliver us, O LORD, we beg you, hear us, O Son.**

Priest: We beg you, hear us, that you may grant peace.

People: **We beg you, hear us, Lamb of God, who takes away the sins of the world, have mercy on us.**

Priest: Christ, hear us.

People: **Christ, hear us.**

Priest: Christ, hear us.

Prayer of St. Ambrose

Priest: Before the sight of your divine Majesty, O God, I stand daring to invoke your holy Name. Have mercy on me, O LORD, a sinful man, clinging to the impure mud. Forgive this unworthy Priest through whose hands this offering seems to be presented. Spare me, O LORD, tainted by the stain of sins, especially those of a grave nature, and do not enter into judgment with your servant, for no one living is justified in your sight. Burdened by the desires and wills of the flesh, we beseech you, O LORD, to remember that we are mere flesh and there is no other to be compared to you in your sight. For these, your servants: *Here the Priest commemorates the names of the deceased.*

Priest: We entreat you to grant them indulgence in light and peace.

Priest: To us sinners also, your servants, who hope for the multitude of your mercies, deign to grant some part and fellowship with your Holy Apostles and Martyrs: with Peter, Paul, Patrick; John, Stephen, Matthias, Barnabas, Ignatius, Alexander, Marcellinus, Peter, Perpetua, Agnes, Cecilia, Felicity, Anastasia, Agatha, Lucia, and with all your Saints; within whose fellowship we beseech you to admit us, not considering our merit but granting us forgiveness, through Jesus Christ our LORD, through whom, O LORD, +create, +sanctify, +renew, +bless, and bestow all these good things upon us. Through +Him, and with +Him, and in +Him, in the unity of the Holy Spirit, all honor and glory is yours, God the Father Almighty, now and ever, and unto the Ages of ages. **Amen.**

Priest: Let your mercy be upon us, O LORD, as we have hoped in you.

Choir and People: **They have known the LORD, alleluia,**

in the breaking of the bread, alleluia.

The bread which we break is the Body of our LORD Jesus Christ, alleluia.

The cup that we bless, alleluia,

is the Blood of our LORD Jesus Christ, alleluia,

for the remission of our sins. Alleluia.

May your mercy, O LORD, be upon us, alleluia,

as we have hoped in you, alleluia.

They have known the LORD, alleluia.

Priest: We believe, O LORD. We believe that we are redeemed in this breaking of the Body and pouring forth of the Blood; we shall rely on the reception of this Sacrament for our fortification, we may enjoy in the true fruits of heaven; through Jesus Christ our LORD, who lives with you and the Holy Spirit, now and forever, and unto the ages of ages. **Amen.**

Divine Prayer

Priest: Having been taught by divine instruction and shaped by divine institution, we dare to say:

People: **Our Father in heaven, hallowed be your Name; your kingdom come, your will be done, on earth as it is in heaven. Give us today our substantial bread. Forgive us our debts as we forgive our debtors. Keep us from falling into temptation and deliver us from evil.**

Priest: For yours is the kingdom, and the power, and the glory of the Father, and the Son, and Holy Spirit, now and ever, and unto the ages of ages. **Amen.**

Priest: Deliver us, O LORD, from every evil, past, present, and future, and through the intercessions of your blessed Apostles Peter, Paul, and Patrick, grant us your gracious peace in our days, that assisted by the aid of your mercy we may always be free from sin and secure from every distress; through Jesus Christ our LORD, who lives with you and the Holy Spirit, now and forever, and unto the ages of ages. **Amen.**

The Offering of Peace

Priest: May the peace and love of our LORD Jesus Christ, and the Communion of all the Saints be with us always.

People: **And with your spirit.**

Priest: You commanded peace, you gave us peace, you left us peace: O LORD, grant us your peace from heaven and may you make this day and the rest of the days of our life peaceful; through Jesus Christ our LORD, who lives with you and the Holy Spirit, now and forever, and unto the ages of ages. **Amen.**

Priest: May the mixing of the Body and Blood of our LORD Jesus Christ be for us salvation unto eternal life. **Amen.**

The Confraction

While the litany is sung, the Priest recites Psalms 22, 23, 24, and 42 in a low voice.

Priest: Behold the Lamb of God; behold him who takes away the sins of the world.

Choir and People: **My peace I give to you, alleluia.**
My peace I leave with you, alleluia.
Abundant peace is for those who are attentive to your law, O LORD, alleluia,
and there is no stumbling for them, alleluia.
For the King of Heaven with peace, alleluia.
Who is full of the promise of life, alleluia.
Sing to him a new song, alleluia.
All you Saints come forth, alleluia.

Come, eat my bread, alleluia,

and drink the wine which had been mixed for you, alleluia.

Whoever eats my body and drinks my blood, alleluia,

Shall abide in me, and I in him, alleluia.

This is the Bread of Life that came down from heaven, alleluia,

whoever eats from it will live forever. Alleluia.

The LORD gave them the bread of heaven. Alleluia,

Man ate the bread of angels. Alleluia.

Eat, my friends, alleluia,

and be intoxicated, my beloved, alleluia.

Take this sacred body and blood of the LORD and Savior,
alleluia,

for yourselves unto eternal life, alleluia.

Upon my lips, I will meditate on a hymn, alleluia,

which you taught me, alleluia,

and I will respond with righteousness, alleluia.

I shall bless the LORD at all times, alleluia.

His praise shall always be in my mouth, alleluia.

Taste and see, alleluia,

how sweet the LORD is, alleluia.

Where I shall be, alleluia,

there also will be my minister, alleluia.

Allow the little ones to come to me, alleluia,

and do not hinder them, alleluia.

For of such is the kingdom of heaven, alleluia.

Devote yourselves to penitence, alleluia,

for the kingdom of heaven is at hand, alleluia.

The kingdom of heaven suffers violence, alleluia.

And the violent take it by force, alleluia.

Come forth and take possession of the kingdom of my Father,
alleluia.

Which has been prepared for you since the beginning of the
world, alleluia.

Postcommunion Prayer

Priest: We have received, O LORD, the heavenly sacrifice celebrating the solemnities of your Saints: We pray that you grant what we do in this temporal life that we may obtain eternal joys; through Jesus Christ our LORD, who lives with you and the Holy Spirit, now and forever, and unto the ages of ages. **Amen.**

The Dismissal

Priest: The Mass has been celebrated in peace.

People: **Amen, thanks be to God.**

The Order of Mass for Living Penitents

Introit

The litany of the apostles and martyrs of the confessors and virgins begins with the people standing

Priest: O God, make speed to save us.

People: **O LORD, make haste to help us.**

Priest: Glory be to the Father, and to the Son, and the Holy Spirit, as it was, as it is, as it shall be through the ages of ages. **Amen.**

Priest: We have sinned, O LORD, we have sinned, spare us our sins, and save us; you who guided Noah over the flood waves, hear us; who with your word recalled Jonah from the abyss, deliver us; who stretched forth your hand to Peter as he sank, help us, O Christ. Son of God, you accomplished marvelous things of the LORD with our fathers, be favorable in our days also; Stretch forth your hand from on high.

Priest: Deliver us, O Christ.

People: **Hear us, O Christ.**

Priest: Hear us, O Christ.

People: **Hear us, O LORD have mercy.**

Priest: Son of God, you who did marvelous things of the LORD with our fathers, be favorable in our days also; Stretch forth your hand from on high. Deliver us, O Christ.

People: **Hear us, O Christ.**

Saint Mary, **pray for us.**

Saint Peter, **pray for us.**

Saint Paul, **pray for us.**

Saint Andrew, **pray for us.**

Saint James, **pray for us.**

Saint Bartholomew, **pray for us.**

Saint Thomas, **pray for us.**

Saint Matthew, **pray for us.**

Saint James, **pray for us.**

Saint Madianus, **pray for us.**

Saint Mark, **pray for us.**

Saint Luke, **pray for us.**

All the Holy Saints, **pray for us.**

Prayer of St. Augustine

All our righteousnesses are unclean like a filthy rag. O Jesus Christ, we are unworthy that we may be living, but you who does not want the death of sinners; grant us forgiveness who are made of flesh so that through the labors of penance we may enjoy eternal life in heaven; through Christ our LORD who reigns with you and the Holy Spirit, now and ever, and unto the ages of ages. **Amen.**

Priest: May our prayer ascend to the throne of your glory, O LORD, and may our request not be returned to us in vain; we ask of this through our LORD Jesus Christ, who lives with you and the Holy Spirit, now and forever, and unto the ages of ages. **Amen.**

Priest: Being pious to your exalted divine Fatherhood, we beseech you in trembling supplication on behalf of your servants: Grant them purity of mind, virtue in deeds, discipline in manners, and may their minds be unwavering in fear of your righteousness; For N., we offer the intention of our devotion to you that they may come to know your mercy; through Jesus Christ our LORD, who lives with you and the Holy Spirit, now and forever, and unto the ages of ages. **Amen.**

The Angelic Hymn

Gloria in Excelsis Deo

Glory to God in the highest,
and on earth peace to people of good will.
We praise you,
we bless you,
we adore you,
we glorify you,
we give you thanks for your great glory,
LORD God, heavenly King,
O God almighty Father.
LORD Jesus Christ, Only Begotten Son,
LORD God, Lamb of God, Son of The Father,
you take away the sins of the world,
have mercy on us;
you take away the sins of the world,
receive our prayer;
you are seated at the right hand of the Father
have mercy on us.
For you alone are the Holy One,
you alone are the LORD,
you alone are the Most High,

Jesus Christ,

with the Holy Spirit,

in the glory of God the Father.

Amen.

Priest: O LORD, indulge us, your penitent servants, as we seek with secure minds to offer you, O LORD our God, a victim for them, N.: May they obtain forgiveness through their devout words, having obtained health through you, Holy Father, may they reach the salvation of eternal grace with your help; through Jesus Christ our LORD, who lives with you and the Holy Spirit, now and forever, and unto the ages of ages. **Amen.**

Priest: We ask that you perfect the desires of their hearts. Almighty One, grant indulgence to those who supplicate, forgiveness to those who request, and fulfill the vows of those who seek. Protect their names by the God of Jacob, command assistance for them from the holy ones and from Zion. For you, O merciful God, consider their sacrifices and offerings before the assembly of Saints.

The Amplification

O God, who by ruling us, preserves us by sparing and justifying us: Deliver us from temporal tribulation and grant us eternal joys; through Jesus Christ our LORD, who lives with you and the Holy Spirit, now and forever, and unto the ages of ages. **Amen.**

Lesson Reading

The people sit. The appointed lesson is read by the Reader.

Here is the First Lesson.

Reader: The word of the LORD.

People: **Amen, thanks be to God.**

Priest: Almighty God for ever and ever, who redeemed your people from the works of the devil with the Blood of your Only-Begotten: Break the bonds of sin, so that those who are drawn to eternal life in the confession of your Name owe nothing to the author of death; through Jesus Christ our LORD, who lives with you and the Holy Spirit, now and forever, and unto the ages of ages. **Amen.**

The Gradual

Here is the Psalm; the last verse is treated as an antiphon. The people stand.

Priest: May the gifts by which the mysteries of our freedom and life are celebrated be pleasing to you, O LORD; through Jesus Christ our LORD, who lives with you and the Holy Spirit, now and forever, and unto the ages of ages. **Amen. Alleluia.**

The Sequence

Here is the Sequence.

Priest: O LORD, we ask that you be appeased by this sacrifice that our devotions may let us proceed to salvation; through Jesus Christ our LORD, who lives with you and the Holy Spirit, now and forever, and unto the ages of ages. **Amen.**

The Litany of St. Martin

Priest: Let us all say, "O LORD, hear us and have mercy upon us. O LORD, have mercy" with all our heart and mind.

Priest: With all our heart and with all our mind, to you who looks upon the earth and makes it tremble, let us pray:

People: **O LORD, hear us and have mercy upon us. O LORD, have mercy.**

Priest: For the most profound peace and tranquility of our times; for the holy catholic Church, which is from one end of the earth to the other, let us pray:

People: **O LORD, hear us and have mercy upon us. O LORD, have mercy.**

Priest: For the Pastor and Bishop N., and for all the bishops, priests, deacons, and all the clergy, let us pray:

People: **O LORD, hear us and have mercy upon us. O LORD, have mercy.**

Priest: For this place and those who dwell in it, for the world's leaders and all the nations' armies, let us pray:

People: **O LORD, hear us and have mercy upon us. O LORD, have mercy.**

Priest: For all those who have been ordained in exaltation for virgins, widows and orphans, let us pray:

People: **O LORD, hear us and have mercy upon us. O LORD, have mercy.**

Priest: For pilgrims and travelers by land, water, air, and space, penitents, and catechumens, let us pray:

People: **O LORD, hear us and have mercy upon us. O LORD, have mercy.**

Priest: For these who in the holy Church give the fruits of mercy, O LORD God of virtue, hear our prayers, we pray:

People: **O LORD, hear us and have mercy upon us. O LORD, have mercy.**

Priest: Let us be mindful of the Saints, Apostles and Martyrs, that by their prayers for us we may receive forgiveness, we pray:

People: **O LORD, hear us and have mercy upon us. O LORD, have mercy.**

Priest: We beseech the LORD to grant us a Christian and peaceful end:

People: **Grant it, O LORD, grant it.**

Priest: We beseech the LORD that the holy bond of Charity may continue in us:

People: **Grant it, O LORD, grant it.**

Priest: We beseech the LORD to preserve the sanctity and the purity of the catholic faith:

People: **Grant it, O LORD, grant it.**

Priest: Let us pray:

People: **O LORD have mercy.**

The Collect after the Litany

O LORD, graciously attend the celebration of this sacrifice to you, which may cleanse us from the sins of our condition and restore us to acceptability in your Name, through Jesus Christ our LORD, who lives with you and the Holy Spirit, now and forever, and unto the ages of ages. **Amen.**

Another

Before your eyes, O LORD, I stand while accused by the witness of a guilty conscience. I do not ask for others that I do not deserve to obtain. O LORD, forgive those who confess, those who sin, those who call upon you for forgiveness, for in your sacrament my perception is infirmed. Grant O LORD, you who does not receive our words with a hard heart that, through you, may mercy be granted;

through Jesus Christ our LORD, who lives with you and the Holy Spirit, now and forever, and unto the ages of ages. **Amen.**

Priest: Let my prayer be set forth in your sight as incense and let the lifting up of my hands be as an evening sacrifice. *Sung three times.*

Priest: Come, O LORD, the almighty sanctifier, and bless this sacrifice prepared for you. *Sung three times.*

The Prayer of St. Gregory

We beseech you, O LORD Almighty God, to graciously look upon our prayers offered to you and extend the right hand of your Majesty to our defense; through Jesus Christ our LORD, who lives with you and the Holy Spirit, now and forever, and unto the ages of ages. **Amen.**

Gospel Lesson

Priest: The Gospel of our LORD according to Saint N.

People: **Glory be to you, O LORD.**

Here is the Gospel reading.

Priest: Pray for us and lift up the Gospel towards us.

The Sermon

The Sermon is given here. The people sit.

Symbol of Faith

Priest and People: **We believe in one God, the Father Almighty, maker of heaven and earth, of all things seen and unseen; we** believe in one **LORD Jesus Christ, the only-begotten Son of God, born from the Father before all ages, light from light, true God from true God, begotten, not made, of one being with the Father, through whom all things were made; who for us and for our salvation He came down from heaven, and was incarnate by the Holy Spirit of the Virgin Mary, and became man; and was crucified for us under Pontius Pilate; he suffered and was buried; and on the third day he rose again, according to the Scriptures; and ascended into heaven, and sits at the right hand of the Father; He will come again with glory to judge the living and the dead; of whose kingdom there will be no end; We believe in the Holy Spirit, the Lord and giver of life, who proceeds from the Father, who with the Father and the Son is worshipped and glorified, who has spoken through the prophets; we believe in one holy Church, catholic and apostolic. We confess one baptism for the remission of sins; we look for the resurrection of the dead and the life of the world to come. Amen.**

Priest: O LORD, show us your mercy and grant us your salvation. *Sung three times.*

The Elevation

Priest: O LORD, sanctify the gifts offered to you and cleanse us from the stains of our sins; through Jesus Christ our LORD, who lives with you and the Holy Spirit, now and forever, and unto the ages of ages. **Amen.**

O LORD, we beseech you to accept these offerings of our devotion, and through the glorious sacrifice of your subjects purify our hearts; through Jesus Christ our LORD, who lives with you and the Holy Spirit, now and forever, and unto the ages of ages. **Amen.**

May these offerings of your people be acceptable to you, O LORD, which we offer in honor of our LORD Jesus Christ, who suffered for us and on the third day rose from the dead; for the souls of our loved ones N. and N.; of our dear ones whose names we recite; and whose names we do not recite but are recited by you in the Book of Eternal Life; of your mercy, rescue them who reigns now and forever, and unto the ages of ages. **Amen.**

The second part is added over the Offerings.

Collect of the Preface

Priest: Almighty God, we again beseech you with our supplications in the presence of your Majesty, especially for your servants N.: We offer this sacrifice for their sins in honor of your Saints: Mary, Peter, Paul, John, and all your Saints. Fulfill their vows so that their petitions may ascend to your merciful ears, that a compassionate blessing may descend upon them, so that they may be protected in all things under the shadow of your wings; through your mercy, may our prayers not be rejected from the presence of your compassion, but deign to assist and defend them in all things; through Jesus Christ our LORD, who lives with you and the Holy Spirit, now and forever, and unto the ages of ages. **Amen.**

Holy Communion

Priest: Lift up your hearts.

People: **We lift them up to the LORD.**

Priest: Let us give thanks to the LORD our God.

People: **It is meet and right.**

Priest: It is truly meet and right, through our LORD Jesus Christ your Son, whose power is to intercede, whose mercy is to entreat, and whose faith to all-encompassing: For who can consider all the miracles of your power, which neither the ears of man can hear, nor ascend into the heart of man, nor can the estimation of men discover the greatness you have prepared for your holy Elect? Yet, being miserable and of earthly imperfection, seek forgiveness not from our merits but from your mercy, pleading for pardon and refuge; in the remembrance of the Saints, through whose intercession we hope for forgiveness, grant to your servants N., the remission of sins that you may perfect their works and answer their needs; finally, through the intercession of your holy Saints, provide these people a remedy for their souls; through Jesus Christ our LORD, who lives with you and the Holy Spirit, now and forever, and unto the ages of ages. **Amen.**

Priest: Through whom the Angels praise your Majesty, the Dominions adore you, the Powers of Heaven tremble, and the Virtues and the blessed Seraphim unite in triumphant chorus to celebrate your Majesty. With whom we entreat you to bid our voices to be admitted as we acclaim:

Sanctus

Choir and People: **Holy, Holy, Holy, LORD God of Sabaoth. Heaven and the whole earth are full of your glory, Hosanna in the highest. Blessed is he who came in the Name of the LORD; Hosanna in the highest.**

Priest: Blessed is He who came from heaven that He might dwell on earth, was made man to destroy the sins of the flesh, became a sacrifice through His passion to give eternal life to those that believe; through Jesus Christ our LORD, who lives with you and the Holy Spirit, now and forever, and unto the ages of ages. **Amen.**

Canon of Pope Gelasius

Priest: Therefore, most merciful Father, through Jesus Christ your son our LORD: We beseech you, and we ask you to accept and bless these gifts, these offerings, these holy sacrifices, which first of all we offer to you for your holy catholic Church; that you may keep her in peace, to guard, unify, and govern her throughout the whole world together with to your most blessed servants, our Patriarchs, Bishops, and to all orthodox and apostolic worshipers of the faith, and to our Metropolitan N. and Bishop N.; remember also, O LORD, your servants and maidens N. and N., (*Names of the living are recited here*) and all those present here, whose faith and devotion is known to you, who offer you this sacrifice of praise, for themselves and for all of theirs; for the redemption of their souls; for their body of elders and of all his ministers; for the integrity of virgins and the continence of widows; for the temperature of the air; and the fruitfulness of the earth; for the return of peace and an end to conflicts; for the safety of our leaders and the peace of the people; and the return of captives and for the prayers of those present today; for the commemoration of martyrs; for the forgiveness of our sins and the correction of their deeds; for the repose of the dead; and the purity of our journey; for the Patriarch, Bishop and all the Bishops, Priests, and all in Holy Orders; for all Christian leaders; for our brothers and sisters; for our brethren who follow the right way; for our brethren whom the LORD has deigned to bring out of the murky darkness of this world, may divine mercy receive them in the eternal rest of the highest light; for our brethren who are afflicted with various sorrows, may the divine mercy take care of them for the hope of their salvation and integrity.

The Nativity of the Lord

And celebrating this most Holy day, on which pure virginity brought forth the Savior into this world;

The Feast of the Circumcision

And celebrating the most holy day of the circumcision of our LORD Jesus Christ;

Epiphany

And celebrating the most holy day of the Supper of our LORD Jesus Christ;

Easter

And the most holy night *or* day of the Resurrection of our LORD Jesus Christ;

The Closing of Easter

And celebrating the most holy day of the end of the Passover of our LORD Jesus Christ;

Ascension

And celebrating the most holy day of the Ascension of our LORD Jesus Christ;

Pentecost

And celebrating the most holy day of the Pentecost of our LORD Jesus Christ on which the Holy Spirit descended upon the Apostles;

Priest: And venerating the memory, first of all, of the glorious Ever-Virgin Mary, the Mother of God and our LORD Jesus Christ, and to your blessed Apostles and martyrs: Peter and Paul, Andrew, James, John, Thomas, James, Philip, Bartholomew, Matthew, Simon and Thaddeus, Anne, Clement, Cornelius, Cyprian, Laurence, Chrysoginus, John, Paul, Cosmas, and Damian, and of all your Saints by whose merits and prayers that you may grant us, that we may be strengthened with the help of your protection in all things; through Jesus Christ our LORD, who lives with you and the Holy Spirit, now and forever, and unto the ages of ages. **Amen.**

Priest: Therefore we offer this oblation of our servitude and of your whole family, which we offer to you in honor of our LORD Jesus Christ, and in commemoration of your blessed martyrs in this church, which your servants built in honor of your glorious Name; through Jesus Christ our LORD, who lives with you and the Holy Spirit, now and forever, and unto the ages of ages. **Amen.**

Priest: Order our days in your peace, deliver us from eternal damnation, and number us among Your Elect; through Jesus Christ our LORD, who lives with you and the Holy Spirit, now and forever, and unto the ages of ages. **Amen.**

Priest: Which offering to you, O God, we beseech you to be pleased in all things to make blessed, ratified, reasonable and acceptable, and to make us worthy to become the Body and Blood of your most beloved Son, our LORD Jesus Christ, who on the day before he suffered, took bread into His holy and venerable hands, He gave thanks to you, he blessed, broke it, and gave it to his disciples, saying, "Take and eat from this, all of you, for this is my Body." In the same way after He had eaten, He took this excellent cup into his holy and venerable hands. Also, giving thanks to you, He blessed it and gave it to his disciples, saying, "Take and drink from this, all of you, for this is the holy chalice of my Blood, of the new and eternal testament, the mystery of faith, which is shed for you and for many in the remission of sins. Whenever you do these things in memory of me, you will preach my passion, announce my resurrection, and hope for my coming until I come to you again from heaven."

Priest: Wherefore, O LORD, we your servants, together with your holy people, remember the blessed passion and death of Christ your Son our LORD, of his resurrection from hell and glorious ascension into heaven: We offer unto your excellent majesty of your own gifts and bounty, to accept them as you have deigned to receive the gifts of your righteous son Abel, and the sacrifice of our patriarch Abraham, and the Holy Sacrifice, the Spotless Host, that your high priest Melchizedek offered to you. We beseech and pray to you, Almighty God to command these things to be carried out by the hands of your holy angel to your sublime altar, in the presence of your divine Majesty, that as many of us as we have taken from this altar of sanctification the sacred Body and Blood of your Most Holy Son, may be filled with all blessings and grace.

Priest: Remember also, O LORD, those who have gone before us with the sign of faith and rest in the peace of Christ, N. With all throughout the whole world who offer the spiritual sacrifices to God the Father, and the Son, and the Holy Spirit, our senior, the Priest N. with the holy and venerable Priests, offers for himself, for his own, and for the whole assembly of the catholic Church; and in commemoration of the wrestling of the venerable Patriarchs, Prophets, Apostles, Martyrs, and of all the Saints, that they may deign to intercede for us before the LORD our God:

Saint Stephen, **pray for us.**

Saint Martin, **pray for us.**

Saint Jerome, **pray for us.**

Saint Augustine, **pray for us.**

Saint Gregory, **pray for us.**

Saint Hilary, **pray for us.**

Saint Patrick, **pray for us.**

Saint Ailbe, **pray for us.**

Saint Finnian, **pray for us.**

Saint Finnian, **pray for us.**

Saint Ciaran, **pray for us.**

Saint Ciaran, **pray for us.**

Saint Brendan, **pray for us.**

Saint Brendan, **pray for us.**

Saint Columba, **pray for us.**

Saint Columba, **pray for us.**

Saint Comgall, **pray for us.**

Saint Cainnech, **pray for us.**

Saint Finbar, **pray for us.**

Saint Nessan, **pray for us.**

Saint Fachtna, **pray for us.**

Saint Lua, **pray for us.**

Saint Lacten, **pray for us.**

Saint Ruadhan, pray for us.

Saint Carthage, **pray for us.**

Saint Kevin, **pray for us.**

Saint Mochoemog, **pray for us.**

Saint Brigid, **pray for us.**

Saint Ite, **pray for us.**

Saint Scetha, **pray for us.**

Saint Sinecha, **pray for us.**

Saint Samthann, **pray for us.**

Priest: All you Saints,

People: **pray for us.**

Priest: Be propitious to us, O LORD, spare us.

People: **Be propitious to us, O LORD, deliver us from all evil.**

Priest: Deliver us, O LORD, through your cross.

People: **Deliver us, O LORD, we beg you, hear us, O Son.**

Priest: We beg you, hear us, that you may grant peace.

People: **We beg you, hear us, Lamb of God, who takes away the sins of the world, have mercy on us.**

Priest: Christ, hear us.

People: **Christ, hear us.**

Priest: Christ, hear us.

Prayer of St. Ambrose

Priest: Before the sight of your divine majesty, O God, I stand daring to invoke your holy Name. Have mercy on me, O LORD, a sinful man, clinging to the impure mud. Forgive this unworthy Priest through whose hands this offering seems to be presented. Spare me, O LORD, tainted by the stain of sins, especially those of a grave nature, and do not enter into judgment with your servant, for no one living is justified in your sight. Burdened by the desires and wills of the flesh, we beseech you, O LORD, to remember that we are mere flesh and there is no other to be compared to you in your sight. For these, your servants: *Here the Priest commemorates the names of the deceased.*

Priest: We entreat you to grant them indulgence in light and peace.

Priest: To us sinners also, your servants, who hope for the multitude of your mercies, deign to grant some part and fellowship with your Holy Apostles and Martyrs: with Peter, Paul, Patrick; John, Stephen, Matthias, Barnabas, Ignatius, Alexander, Marcellinus, Peter, Perpetua, Agnes, Cecilia, Felicity, Anastasia, Agatha, Lucia, and with all your Saints; within whose fellowship we beseech you to admit us, not considering our merit but granting us forgiveness, through Jesus Christ our LORD, through whom, O LORD, +create, +sanctify, +renew, +bless, and bestow all these good things upon us. Through +Him, and with +Him, and in +Him, in the unity of the Holy Spirit, all honor and glory is yours, God the Father Almighty, now and ever, and unto the Ages of ages. **Amen.**

Priest: Let your mercy be upon us, O LORD, as we have hoped in you.

Choir and People: **They have known the LORD, alleluia,**
in the breaking of the bread, alleluia.
The bread which we break is the Body of our LORD
  Jesus Christ, alleluia.
The cup that we bless, alleluia,
is the Blood of our LORD Jesus Christ, alleluia,
for the remission of our sins. Alleluia.
May your mercy, O LORD, be upon us, alleluia,
as we have hoped in you, alleluia.
They have known the LORD, alleluia.

Priest: We believe, O LORD. We believe that we are redeemed in this breaking of the Body and pouring forth of the Blood; we shall rely on the reception of this Sacrament for our fortification, we may enjoy in the true fruits of heaven; through Jesus Christ our LORD, who lives with you and the Holy Spirit, now and forever, and unto the ages of ages. **Amen.**

Divine Prayer

Priest: Having been taught by divine instruction and shaped by divine institution, we dare to say:

People: **Our Father in heaven, hallowed be your Name; your kingdom come, your will be done, on earth as it is in heaven. Give us today our substantial bread. Forgive us our debts as we forgive our debtors. Keep us from falling into temptation and deliver us from evil.**

Priest: For yours is the kingdom, and the power, and the glory of the Father, and the Son, and Holy Spirit, now and ever, and unto the ages of ages. **Amen.**

Priest: Deliver us, O LORD, from every evil, past, present, and future, and through the intercessions of your blessed Apostles Peter, Paul, and Patrick, grant us your gracious peace in our days, that assisted by the aid of your mercy we may always be free from sin and secure from every distress; through Jesus Christ our LORD, who lives with you and the Holy Spirit, now and forever, and unto the ages of ages. **Amen.**

The Offering of Peace

Priest: May the peace and love of our LORD Jesus Christ, and the Communion of all the Saints be with us always.

People: **And with your spirit.**

Priest: You commanded peace, you gave us peace, you left us peace: O LORD, grant us your peace from heaven and may you make this day and the rest of the days of our life peaceful; through Jesus Christ our LORD, who lives with you and the Holy Spirit, now and forever, and unto the ages of ages. **Amen.**

Priest: May the mixing of the Body and Blood of our LORD Jesus Christ be for us salvation unto eternal life. **Amen.**

The Confraction

While the litany is sung, the Priest recites Psalms 22, 23, 24, and 42 in a low voice.

Priest: Behold the Lamb of God; behold him who takes away the sins of the world.

Choir and People: **My peace I give to you, alleluia.**

My peace I leave with you, alleluia.

Abundant peace is for those who are attentive to your law, O LORD, alleluia,

and there is no stumbling for them, alleluia.

For the King of Heaven with peace, alleluia.

Who is full of the promise of life, alleluia.

Sing to him a new song, alleluia.

All you Saints come forth, alleluia.

Come, eat my bread, alleluia,

and drink the wine which had been mixed for you, alleluia.

Whoever eats my body and drinks my blood, alleluia,

Shall abide in me, and I in him, alleluia.

This is the Bread of Life that came down from heaven, alleluia, whoever eats from it will live forever. Alleluia.

The LORD gave them the bread of heaven. Alleluia, Man ate the bread of angels. Alleluia.

Eat, my friends, alleluia, and be intoxicated, my beloved, alleluia.

Take this sacred body and blood of the LORD and Savior, alleluia,

for yourselves unto eternal life, alleluia.

Upon my lips, I will meditate on a hymn, alleluia,

which you taught me, alleluia,

and I will respond with righteousness, alleluia.

I shall bless the LORD at all times, alleluia.

His praise shall always be in my mouth, alleluia.

Taste and see, alleluia,

how sweet the LORD is, alleluia.

Where I shall be, alleluia,

there also will be my minister, alleluia.

Allow the little ones to come to me, alleluia,

and do not hinder them, alleluia.

For of such is the kingdom of heaven, alleluia.

Devote yourselves to penitence, alleluia,

for the kingdom of heaven is at hand, alleluia.

The kingdom of heaven suffers violence, alleluia.

And the violent take it by force, alleluia.

Come forth and take possession of the kingdom of my Father, alleluia.

Which has been prepared for you since the beginning of the world, alleluia.

Priest: O God, who purifies the hearts of those who confess to you and absolves those who accuse their consciences from all iniquities: Grant forgiveness to the sinners, provide healing to the wounded, and the remission of all sins through the reception of your Sacraments, that they may endure through sincere dedication, and not suffer any harm to their eternal redemption; through Jesus Christ our LORD, who lives with you and the Holy Spirit, now and forever, and unto the ages of ages. **Amen.**

Postcommunion Prayer

We give thanks to you, O LORD, Holy Father, Almighty and eternal God, who has satisfied us by the Communion of the Body and Blood of Christ your Son: We humbly implore for your mercy, that this your Sacrament may not bring condemnation unto punishment, but may be an intercession for salvation, a remission of sins, a strengthening for the weak, a defense against the dangers of the world; may this Communion purify us from our faults and grant us to be participants in heavenly joy; through Jesus Christ our LORD, who lives with you and the Holy Spirit, now and forever, and unto the ages of ages. **Amen.**

The Dismissal

Priest: The Mass has been celebrated in peace.

People: **Amen, thanks be to God.**

The Order of Mass for All Dead

Introit

The litany of the apostles and martyrs of the confessors and virgins begins with the people standing

Priest: O God, make speed to save us.

People: **O LORD, make haste to help us.**

Priest: Glory be to the Father, and to the Son, and the Holy Spirit, as it was, as it is, as it shall be through the ages of ages. **Amen.**

Priest: We have sinned, O LORD, we have sinned, spare us our sins, and save us; You who guided Noah over the flood waves, hear us; who with your word recalled Jonah from the abyss, deliver us; who stretched forth your hand to Peter as he sank, help us, O Christ. Son of God, you accomplished marvelous things of the LORD with our fathers, be favorable in our days also; Stretch forth your hand from on high.

Priest: Deliver us, O Christ.

People: **Hear us, O Christ.**

Priest: Hear us, O Christ.

People: **Hear us, O LORD have mercy.**

Priest: Son of God, you who did marvelous things of the LORD with our fathers, be favorable in our days also; Stretch forth your hand from on high. Deliver us, O Christ.

People: **Hear us, O Christ.**

Saint Mary, **pray for us.**

Saint Peter, **pray for us.**

Saint Paul, **pray for us.**

Saint Andrew, **pray for us.**

Saint James, **pray for us.**

Saint Bartholomew, **pray for us.**

Saint Thomas, **pray for us.**

Saint Matthew, **pray for us.**

Saint James, **pray for us.**

Saint Madianus, **pray for us.**

Saint Mark, **pray for us.**

Saint Luke, **pray for us.**

All the Holy Saints, **pray for us.**

Prayer of St. Augustine

All our righteousnesses are unclean like a filthy rag. O Jesus Christ, we are unworthy that we may be living, but you who does not want the death of sinners; grant us forgiveness who are made of flesh so that through the labors of penance we may enjoy eternal life in heaven; through Christ our LORD who reigns with you and the Holy Spirit, now and ever, and unto the ages of ages. **Amen.**

Priest: May our prayer ascend to the throne of your glory, O LORD, and may our request not be returned to us in vain; we ask of this through our LORD Jesus Christ, who lives with you and the Holy Spirit, now and forever, and unto the ages of ages. **Amen.**

Priest: We beseech you, Almighty and merciful God, to grant that the souls of your servants N. may find the forgiveness of their sins and the eternal splendor of light; through Jesus Christ our LORD, who lives with you and the Holy Spirit, now and forever, and unto the ages of ages. **Amen.**

The Angelic Hymn

Gloria in Excelsis Deo

Glory to God in the highest,
and on earth peace to people of good will.
We praise you,
we bless you,
we adore you,
we glorify you,
we give you thanks for your great glory,
LORD God, heavenly King,
O God almighty Father.
LORD Jesus Christ, Only Begotten Son,
LORD God, Lamb of God, Son of The Father,
you take away the sins of the world,
have mercy on us;
you take away the sins of the world,
receive our prayer;
you are seated at the right hand of the Father
have mercy on us.
For you alone are the Holy One,
you alone are the LORD,
you alone are the Most High,
Jesus Christ,
with the Holy Spirit,
in the glory of God the Father.
Amen.

For those who turn from God and transgress daily

O God, who has prepared unattainable goods for those devoted to
you, pour forth into our hearts the feeling of your love, so that we
may follow you in all things, and above all things we may pursue

your promises which surpasses all expectations; through Jesus Christ our LORD, who lives with you and the Holy Spirit, now and forever, and unto the ages of ages. **Amen.**

Priest: Bestow upon us your mercy, O LORD, that the souls of your servants N., be purified from all vices and may await the day of future resurrection, freed from all concerns under your protection; through Jesus Christ our LORD, who lives with you and the Holy Spirit, now and forever, and unto the ages of ages. **Amen.**

The Amplification

O God, who by ruling us, preserves us by sparing and justifying us: Deliver us from temporal tribulation and grant us eternal joys; through Jesus Christ our LORD, who lives with you and the Holy Spirit, now and forever, and unto the ages of ages. **Amen.**

Lesson Reading

The people sit. The appointed lesson is read by the Reader.

Here is the First Lesson.

Reader: The word of the LORD.

People: **Amen, thanks be to God.**

Priest: Almighty God for ever and ever, who redeemed your people from the works of the devil with the Blood of your Only-Begotten: Break the bonds of sin, so that those who are drawn to eternal life in the confession of your Name owe nothing to the author of death; through Jesus Christ our LORD, who lives with you and the Holy Spirit, now and forever, and unto the ages of ages. **Amen.**

The Gradual

Here is the Psalm; the last verse is treated as an antiphon. The people stand.

Priest: May the gifts by which the mysteries of our freedom and life are celebrated be pleasing to you, O LORD; through Jesus Christ our LORD, who lives with you and the Holy Spirit, now and forever, and unto the ages of ages. **Amen. Alleluia.**

The Sequence

Here is the Sequence.

Priest: O LORD, we ask that you be appeased by this sacrifice that our devotions may let us proceed to salvation; through Jesus Christ our LORD, who lives with you and the Holy Spirit, now and forever, and unto the ages of ages. **Amen.**

The Litany of St. Martin

Priest: Let us all say, "O LORD, hear us and have mercy upon us. O LORD, have mercy" with all our heart and mind.

Priest: With all our heart and with all our mind, to you who looks upon the earth and makes it tremble, let us pray:

People: **O LORD, hear us and have mercy upon us. O LORD, have mercy.**

Priest: For the most profound peace and tranquility of our times; for the holy catholic Church, which is from one end of the earth to the other, let us pray:

People: **O LORD, hear us and have mercy upon us. O LORD, have mercy.**

Priest: For the Pastor and Bishop N., and for all the bishops, priests, deacons, and all the clergy, let us pray:

People: **O LORD, hear us and have mercy upon us. O LORD, have mercy.**

Priest: For this place and those who dwell in it, for the world's leaders and all the nations' armies, let us pray:

People: **O LORD, hear us and have mercy upon us. O LORD, have mercy.**

Priest: For all those who have been ordained in exaltation for virgins, widows and orphans, let us pray:

People: **O LORD, hear us and have mercy upon us. O LORD, have mercy.**

Priest: For pilgrims and travelers by land, water, air, and space, penitents, and catechumens, let us pray:

People: **O LORD, hear us and have mercy upon us. O LORD, have mercy.**

Priest: For these who in the holy Church give the fruits of mercy, O LORD God of virtue, hear our prayers, we pray:

People: **O LORD, hear us and have mercy upon us. O LORD, have mercy.**

Priest: Let us be mindful of the Saints, Apostles and Martyrs, that by their prayers for us we may receive forgiveness, we pray:

People: **O LORD, hear us and have mercy upon us. O LORD, have mercy.**

Priest: We beseech the LORD to grant us a Christian and peaceful end:

People: **Grant it, O LORD, grant it.**

Priest: We beseech the LORD that the holy bond of Charity may continue in us:

People: **Grant it, O LORD, grant it.**

Priest: We beseech the LORD to preserve the sanctity and the purity of the catholic faith:

People: **Grant it, O LORD, grant it.**

Priest: Let us pray:

People: **O LORD have mercy.**

The Collect after the Litany

O LORD, graciously attend the celebration of this sacrifice to you, which may cleanse us from the sins of our condition and restore us to acceptability in your Name, through Jesus Christ our LORD, who lives with you and the Holy Spirit, now and forever, and unto the ages of ages. **Amen.**

Another

Before your eyes, O LORD, I stand while accused by the witness of a guilty conscience. I do not ask for others that I do not deserve to obtain. O LORD, forgive those who confess, those who sin, those who call upon you for forgiveness, for in your sacrament my perception is infirmed. Grant O LORD, you who does not receive our words with a hard heart that, through you, may mercy be granted; through Jesus Christ our LORD, who lives with you and the Holy Spirit, now and forever, and unto the ages of ages. **Amen.**

Priest: Let my prayer be set forth in your sight as incense and let the lifting up of my hands be as an evening sacrifice. *Sung three times.*

Priest: Come, O LORD, the almighty sanctifier, and bless this sacrifice prepared for you. *Sung three times.*

The Prayer of St. Gregory

We beseech you, O LORD Almighty God, to graciously look upon our prayers offered to you and extend the right hand of your Majesty to our defense; through Jesus Christ our LORD, who lives with you and the Holy Spirit, now and forever, and unto the ages of ages. **Amen.**

Gospel Lesson

Priest: The Gospel of our LORD according to Saint N.

People: **Glory be to You, O LORD.**

Here is the Gospel reading.

Priest: Pray for us and lift up the Gospel towards us.

The Sermon

The Sermon is given here. The people sit.

Symbol of Faith

Priest and People: **We believe in one God, the Father Almighty, maker of heaven and earth, of all things seen and unseen; we believe in one LORD Jesus Christ, the only-begotten Son of God, born from the Father before all ages, light from light, true God from true God, begotten, not made, of one being with the Father, through whom all things were made; who for us and for our salvation He came down from heaven, and was incarnate by the Holy Spirit of the Virgin Mary, and became man; and was crucified for us under Pontius Pilate; he suffered and was buried; and on the third day he rose again, according to the Scriptures; and ascended into heaven, and sits at the right hand of the Father; He will come again with glory to judge the living** and the dead; of whose kingdom there will be no end; We believe in the Holy Spirit, the Lord and giver of life, who proceeds from the Father, who with the Father and the Son is worshipped and glorified, who has spoken through the prophets; we believe in one holy Church, catholic and apostolic. We confess one baptism for the remission of sins; we look for the resurrection of the dead and the life of the world to come. Amen.

Priest: O LORD, show us your mercy and grant us your salvation. *Sung three times.*

The Elevation

Priest: O LORD, sanctify the gifts offered to you and cleanse us from the stains of our sins; through Jesus Christ our LORD, who lives with you and the Holy Spirit, now and forever, and unto the ages of ages. **Amen.**

Priest: O LORD, we beseech you to accept these offerings of our devotion, and through the glorious sacrifice of your subjects purify our hearts; through Jesus Christ our LORD, who lives with you and the Holy Spirit, now and forever, and unto the ages of ages. **Amen.**

Priest: May these offerings of your people be acceptable to you, O LORD, which we offer in honor of our LORD Jesus Christ, who suffered for us and on the third day rose from the dead; for the souls of our loved ones N. and N.; of our dear ones whose names we recite; and whose names we do not recite but are recited by you in the Book of Eternal Life; of your mercy, rescue them who reigns now and forever, and unto the ages of ages. **Amen.**

Collect of the Preface

Attend, O LORD, to the gifts which we bring to your altars in commemoration of your Saints N. and for our offenses; through Jesus

Christ our LORD, who lives with you and the Holy Spirit, now and forever, and unto the ages of ages. **Amen.**

Holy Communion

Priest: Lift up your hearts.

People: **We lift them up to the LORD.**

Priest: Let us give thanks to the LORD our God.

People: **It is meet and right.**

Priest: It is truly meet and right that we await the fulfillment of the promised eternal good things in Him, in whom we know the promises are left with us, Our LORD Jesus Christ, who is the true life of believers: We beseech you on behalf of your servants N., for whom we offer this sacrifice, that you may deem them cleansed by the holy regeneration and exempt from temptations, worthy to be numbered among the Saints; May you grant them to be participants by adoption that you have made them sharers in your inheritance; through Jesus Christ our LORD, who lives with you and the Holy Spirit, now and forever, and unto the ages of ages. **Amen.**

Priest: Through whom the Angels praise your Majesty, the Dominions adore you, the Powers of Heaven tremble, and the Virtues and the blessed Seraphim unite in triumphant chorus to celebrate your Majesty. With whom we entreat you to bid our voices to be admitted as we acclaim:

Sanctus

Choir and People: **Holy, Holy, Holy, LORD God of Sabaoth. Heaven and the whole earth are full of your glory, Hosanna in the highest. Blessed is he who came in the Name of the LORD; Hosanna in the highest.**

Priest: Blessed is He who came from heaven that He might dwell on earth, was made man to destroy the sins of the flesh, became a sacrifice through His passion to give eternal life to those that believe; through Jesus Christ our LORD, who lives with you and the Holy Spirit, now and forever, and unto the ages of ages. **Amen.**

Canon of Pope Gelasius

Priest: Therefore, most merciful Father, through Jesus Christ your son our LORD: We beseech you, and we ask you to accept and bless these gifts, these offerings, these holy sacrifices, which first of all we offer to you for your holy catholic Church; that you may keep her in peace, to guard, unify, and govern her throughout the whole world together with to your most blessed servants, our Patriarchs, Bishops, and to all orthodox and apostolic worshipers of the faith, and to our Metropolitan N. and Bishop N.; remember also, O LORD, your servants and maidens N. and N., (*Names of the living are recited here*) and all those present here, whose faith and devotion is known to you, who offer you this sacrifice of praise, for themselves and for all of theirs; for the redemption of their souls; for their body of elders and of all his ministers; for the integrity of virgins and the continence of widows; for the temperature of the air; and the fruitfulness of the earth; for the return of peace and an end to conflicts; for the safety of our leaders and the peace of the people; and the return of captives and for the prayers of those present today; for the commemoration of martyrs; for the forgiveness of our sins and the correction of their deeds; for the repose of the dead; and the purity of our journey; for the Patriarch, Bishop and all the Bishops, Priests, and all in Holy Orders; for all Christian leaders; for our brothers and sisters; for our brethren who follow the right way; for our brethren whom the LORD has deigned to bring out of the murky darkness of this world, may divine mercy receive them in the eternal rest of the highest light; for our brethren who are afflicted with various sorrows, may the divine mercy take care of them for the hope of their salvation and integrity.

The Nativity of the Lord

And celebrating this most Holy day, on which pure virginity brought forth the Savior into this world;

The Feast of the Circumcision

And celebrating the most holy day of the circumcision of our LORD Jesus Christ;

Epiphany

And celebrating the most holy day of the Supper of our LORD Jesus Christ;

Easter

And the most holy night *or* day of the Resurrection of our LORD Jesus Christ;

The Closing of Easter

And celebrating the most holy day of the end of the Passover of our LORD Jesus Christ;

Ascension

And celebrating the most holy day of the Ascension of our LORD Jesus Christ;

Pentecost

And celebrating the most holy day of the Pentecost of our LORD Jesus Christ on which the Holy Spirit descended upon the Apostles;

Priest: And venerating the memory, first of all, of the glorious Ever-Virgin Mary, the Mother of God and our LORD Jesus Christ, and to your blessed Apostles and martyrs: Peter and Paul, Andrew, James, John, Thomas, James, Philip, Bartholomew, Matthew, Simon and Thaddeus, Anne, Clement, Cornelius, Cyprian, Laurence, Chrysoginus, John, Paul, Cosmas, and Damian, and of all your Saints by whose merits and prayers that you may grant us, that we may be strengthened with the help of your protection in all things; through Jesus Christ our LORD, who lives with you and the Holy Spirit, now and forever, and unto the ages of ages. **Amen.**

Priest: Therefore we offer this oblation of our servitude and of your whole family, which we offer to you in honor of our LORD Jesus Christ, and in commemoration of your blessed martyrs in this church, which your servants built in honor of your glorious Name; through Jesus Christ our LORD, who lives with you and the Holy Spirit, now and forever, and unto the ages of ages. **Amen.**

Priest: Order our days in your peace, deliver us from eternal damnation, and number us among your Elect; through Jesus Christ our LORD, who lives with you and the Holy Spirit, now and forever, and unto the ages of ages. **Amen.**

Priest: Which offering to you, O God, we beseech you to be pleased in all things to make blessed, ratified, reasonable and acceptable, and to make us worthy to become the Body and Blood of your most beloved Son, our LORD Jesus Christ, who on the day before he suffered, took bread into His holy and venerable hands, He gave thanks to you, he blessed, broke it, and gave it to his disciples, saying, "Take and eat from this, all of you, for this is my Body." In the same way after He had eaten, He took this excellent cup into his holy and venerable hands. Also, giving thanks to you, He blessed it and gave it to his disciples, saying, "Take and drink from this, all of you, for this is the holy chalice of my Blood, of the new and eternal testament, the mystery of faith, which is shed for you and for many in the remission of sins. Whenever you do these things in memory of me, you will preach my passion, announce my resurrection, and hope for my coming until I come to you again from heaven."

Priest: Wherefore, O LORD, we your servants, together with your holy people, remember the blessed passion and death of Christ your Son our LORD, of his resurrection from hell and glorious ascension into heaven: We offer unto your excellent majesty of your own gifts and bounty, to accept them as you have deigned to receive the gifts of your righteous son Abel, and the sacrifice of our patriarch Abraham, and the Holy Sacrifice, the Spotless Host, that your high priest Melchizedek offered to you. We beseech and pray to you, Almighty God to command these things to be carried out by the hands of your holy angel to your sublime altar, in the presence of your divine Majesty, that as many of us as we have taken from this altar of sanctification the sacred Body and Blood of your Most Holy Son, may be filled with all blessings and grace.

Priest: Remember also, O LORD, those who have gone before us with the sign of faith and rest in the peace of Christ, N. With all throughout the whole world who offer the spiritual sacrifices to God the Father, and the Son, and the Holy Spirit, our senior, the Priest N. with the holy and venerable Priests, offers for himself, for his own, and for the whole assembly of the catholic Church; and in commemoration of the wrestling of the venerable Patriarchs, Prophets, Apostles, Martyrs, and of all the Saints, that they may deign to intercede for us before the LORD our God:

Saint Stephen, **pray for us.**	Saint Comgall, **pray for us.**
Saint Martin, **pray for us.**	Saint Cainnech, **pray for us.**
Saint Jerome, **pray for us.**	Saint Finbar, **pray for us.**
Saint Augustine, **pray for us.**	Saint Nessan, **pray for us.**
Saint Gregory, **pray for us.**	Saint Fachtna, **pray for us.**
Saint Hilary, **pray for us.**	Saint Lua, **pray for us.**

Saint Patrick, **pray for us.**	Saint Lacten, **pray for us.**
Saint Ailbe, **pray for us.**	Saint Ruadhan, pray for us.
Saint Finnian, **pray for us.**	Saint Carthage, **pray for us.**
Saint Finnian, **pray for us.**	Saint Kevin, **pray for us.**
Saint Ciaran, **pray for us.**	Saint Mochoemog, **pray for us.**
Saint Ciaran, **pray for us.**	Saint Brigid, **pray for us.**
Saint Brendan, **pray for us.**	Saint Ite, **pray for us.**
Saint Brendan, **pray for us.**	Saint Scetha, **pray for us.**
Saint Columba, **pray for us.**	Saint Sinecha, **pray for us.**
Saint Columba, **pray for us.**	Saint Samthann, **pray for us.**

Priest: All you saints,

People: **pray for us.**

Priest: Be propitious to us, O LORD, spare us.

People: **Be propitious to us, O LORD, deliver us from all evil.**

Priest: Deliver us, O LORD, through your cross.

People: **Deliver us, O LORD, we beg you, hear us, O Son.**

Priest: We beg you, hear us, that you may grant peace.

People: **We beg you, hear us, Lamb of God, who takes away the sins of the world, have mercy on us.**

Priest: Christ, hear us.

People: **Christ, hear us.**

Priest: Christ, hear us.

Prayer of St. Ambrose

Priest: Before the sight of your divine majesty, O God, I stand daring to invoke your holy Name. Have mercy on me, O LORD, a sinful man, clinging to the impure mud. Forgive this unworthy Priest through whose hands this offering seems to be presented. Spare me, O LORD, tainted by the stain of sins, especially those of a grave nature, and do not enter into judgment with your servant, for no one living is justified in your sight. Burdened by the desires and wills of the flesh, we beseech you, O LORD, to remember that we are mere flesh and there is no other to be compared to you in your sight. For these, your servants: *Here the Priest commemorates the names of the deceased.*

Priest: We entreat you to grant them indulgence in light and peace.

Priest: To us sinners also, your servants, who hope for the multitude of your mercies, deign to grant some part and fellowship with your Holy Apostles and Martyrs: with Peter, Paul, Patrick; John, Stephen, Matthias, Barnabas, Ignatius, Alexander, Marcellinus, Peter, Perpetua, Agnes, Cecilia, Felicity, Anastasia, Agatha, Lucia, and with all your saints; within whose fellowship we beseech you to admit us, not considering our merit but granting us forgiveness, through Jesus Christ our LORD, through whom, O LORD, +create, +sanctify, +renew, +bless, and bestow all these good things upon us. Through +Him, and with +Him, and in +Him, in the unity of the Holy Spirit, all honor and glory is yours, God the Father Almighty, now and ever, and unto the Ages of ages. **Amen.**

Priest: Let your mercy be upon us, O LORD, as we have hoped in you.

Choir and People: **They have known the LORD, alleluia,**
in the breaking of the bread, alleluia.
The bread which we break is the Body of our LORD Jesus
  Christ, alleluia.
The cup that we bless, alleluia,
is the Blood of our LORD Jesus Christ, alleluia,
for the remission of our sins. Alleluia.
May your mercy, O LORD, be upon us, alleluia,
as we have hoped in you, alleluia.
They have known the LORD, alleluia.

Priest: We believe, O LORD. We believe that we are redeemed in this breaking of the Body and pouring forth of the Blood; we shall rely on the reception of this Sacrament for our fortification, we may enjoy in the true fruits of heaven; through Jesus Christ our LORD, who lives with you and the Holy Spirit, now and forever, and unto the ages of ages. **Amen.**

Divine Prayer

Priest: Having been taught by divine instruction and shaped by divine institution, we dare to say:

People: **Our Father in heaven, hallowed be your Name; your kingdom come, your will be done, on earth as it is in heaven. Give us today our substantial bread. Forgive us our debts as we forgive our debtors. Keep us from falling into temptation and deliver us from evil.**

Priest: For yours is the kingdom, and the power, and the glory of the Father, and the Son, and Holy Spirit, now and ever, and unto the ages of ages. **Amen.**

Priest: Deliver us, O LORD, from every evil, past, present, and future, and through the intercessions of your blessed Apostles Peter, Paul, and Patrick, grant us your gracious peace in our days, that assisted by the aid of your mercy we may always be free from sin and secure from every distress; through Jesus Christ our LORD, who lives with you and the Holy Spirit, now and forever, and unto the ages of ages. **Amen.**

The Offering of Peace

Priest: May the peace and love of our LORD Jesus Christ, and the Communion of all the Saints be with us always.

People: **And with your spirit.**

Priest: You commanded peace, you gave us peace, you left us peace: O LORD, grant us your peace from heaven and may you make this day and the rest of the days of our life peaceful; through Jesus Christ our LORD, who lives with you and the Holy Spirit, now and forever, and unto the ages of ages. **Amen.**

Priest: May the mixing of the Body and Blood of our LORD Jesus Christ be for us salvation unto eternal life. **Amen.**

The Confraction

While the litany is sung, the Priest recites Psalms 22, 23, 24, and 42 in a low voice.

Priest: Behold the Lamb of God; behold him who takes away the sins of the world.

Choir and People: **My peace I give to you, alleluia.**

My peace I leave with you, alleluia.

Abundant peace is for those who are attentive to your law,
   O LORD, alleluia,

and there is no stumbling for them, alleluia.

For the King of Heaven with peace, alleluia.

Who is full of the promise of life, alleluia.

Sing to him a new song, alleluia.

All you Saints come forth, alleluia.

Come, eat my bread, alleluia,

and drink the wine which had been mixed for you, alleluia.

Whoever eats my body and drinks my blood, alleluia,

Shall abide in me, and I in him, alleluia.

This is the Bread of Life that came down from heaven, alleluia,

whoever eats from it will live forever. Alleluia.

The LORD gave them the bread of heaven. Alleluia,

Man ate the bread of angels. Alleluia.

Eat, my friends, alleluia,

and be intoxicated, my beloved, alleluia.

Take this sacred body and blood of the LORD and Savior,
    alleluia,

for yourselves unto eternal life, alleluia.

Upon my lips, I will meditate on a hymn, alleluia,

which you taught me, alleluia,

and I will respond with righteousness, alleluia.

I shall bless the LORD at all times, alleluia.

His praise shall always be in my mouth, alleluia.

Taste and see, alleluia,

how sweet the LORD is, alleluia.

Where I shall be, alleluia,

there also will be my minister, alleluia.

Allow the little ones to come to me, alleluia,

and do not hinder them, alleluia.

For of such is the kingdom of heaven, alleluia.

Devote yourselves to penitence, alleluia,

for the kingdom of heaven is at hand, alleluia.

The kingdom of heaven suffers violence, alleluia.

And the violent take it by force, alleluia.

Come forth and take possession of the kingdom of my Father, alleluia.

Which has been prepared for you since the beginning of the world, alleluia.

Priest: Grant, O LORD, that those whom you have satisfied with heavenly gifts, may be cleansed from their hidden sins and we may be set free from the snares of the enemy. **Amen.**

Postcommunion Prayer

Let us pray, dearest brothers and sisters, for our beloved N., who have already proceeded into the peace of the LORD, his destined end and the conclusion to the order of his transition: May Almighty God, the Father of our LORD Jesus Christ, command his flesh, soul, and spirit to be received into the place of light and place of refreshment, in the bosom of Abraham, Isaac, and Jacob; may He pardon whatever they may have improperly sinned through ignorance and the deceit of the enemy, and may He deign to refresh them with the spirit of His mouth; through Jesus Christ our LORD, who lives with you and the Holy Spirit, now and forever, and unto the ages of ages. **Amen.**

The Dismissal

Priest: The Mass has been celebrated in peace.

People: **Amen, thanks be to God.**

Order of Baptism

The people standing, the Priest says:

O God, who made Adam from the dust of the earth, and although he sinned in paradise, you did not consider him guilty of the punishment of death for his sins, but through the blood of your Only-Begotten Son, you deigned to redeem him and bring him back to Holy Jerusalem: Therefore, O accursed one, acknowledge your sentence, give honor to the living God, and depart from this servant of God; for my God and LORD has deemed it worthy to call this person to his holy grace and mercy through this +Sign of the Cross, so that you, devil, may never approach him; through Christ our LORD who reigns with you and the Holy Spirit, now and ever, and unto the ages of ages.

People: **Amen.**

Priest: O LORD, holy Father, Almighty and everlasting God, expel the devil and heathenism from this person: from the head, from the hair, from the crown, from the brain, from the brow, from the eyes, from the ears, from the nose, from the mouth, from the tongue, from under the tongue, from the throat, from the jaws, from the neck, from the chest, from the heart, from the whole body inside and out, from the hands, from the feet, from all the limbs, from the joints of the limbs, and from the thoughts, words, deeds, and all behaviors now and in the future; Through Christ our LORD who reigns with you and the Holy Spirit, now and ever, and unto the ages of ages.

People: **Amen.**

Order of Baptism

Prayer for Consecration of Water

O God, who has established the greatest Sacrament for the salvation of humanity in the substance of water, be responsive to our invocations and pour forth your blessings, through many modes of purification. Let this creature of water serve the Mystery, becoming effective for casting out demons and expelling diseases. By your divine grace, may it confer that effect so that whoever it touches or wherever it is sprinkled, and in the homes of the faithful, may be free from impurity, released from harm, without the presence of pestilent spirits or corruption of air. May all hidden snares of the enemy be removed, and whatever bears malice to the safety or tranquility of the inhabitants may flee upon the sprinkling of this water, so that healing may be sought through the invocation of your name. Let it defend against every attack, through Christ our LORD who reigns with you and the Holy Spirit, now and ever, and unto the ages of ages.

People: **Amen.**

Alternative Prayer for Consecration of Water

Bless, O LORD, this creature of water, that it may be a healing remedy for humanity: Grant that through the invocation of your name, through this water, the health of the body, the protection of the soul, and the defense of all things; through Christ our LORD who reigns with you and the Holy Spirit, now and ever, and unto the ages of ages.

People: **Amen.**

Prayer for Consecration of Salt

O God, who has provided a medicine through this healing salt, grant that this soul be turned away from the error of heathenism and be redeemed, confessing the Triune God while repelling the devil by the invocation and by the + Sign of the Cross of Jesus Christ our LORD who reigns with you and the Holy Spirit, now and ever, and unto the ages of ages.

People: **Amen.**

Another

I exorcise you, O creature of salt, in the Name of God the Father Almighty, and in the love of our LORD Jesus Christ, and in the power of the Holy Spirit. I exorcise you by the Living God, by the True God, who created you for the protection of humankind and to be consecrated by his servants for the people coming into the Faith. Therefore, we pray to you, O LORD and our God, that this creature of salt in the + Name of the Trinity may become effective for salvation, a Sacrament to drive away the enemy. May it be +sanctified and +blessed by you, O LORD, so that it may serve as an eternal medicine for all, remaining in their innermost being in the name of our LORD Jesus Christ, who will judge the living and the dead and the world by fire.

Amen.

The Abjuration

Priest: Do you renounce Satan?

People: **I renounce him.**

Priest: And all his works?

People: **I renounce them.**

Priest: And all his pomps?

People: **I renounce them.**

The Confession

Priest: Do you believe in God the Almighty Father?

Catechumen: **I believe in God,**
the Father almighty,
Creator of heaven and earth.

Priest: Do you also believe in Jesus Christ?

Catechumen: **I believe in Jesus Christ,**
his only Son, our LORD,
who was conceived by the Holy Spirit,
born of the Virgin Mary,
suffered under Pontius Pilate,
was crucified, died and was buried;
he descended into hell;
on the third day he rose again from the dead;
he ascended into heaven,
and is seated at the right hand of God the Father almighty;
from there he will come to judge the living and the dead.

Priest: Do you also believe in the Holy Spirit?

Catechumen: **I believe in the Holy Spirit,**
the holy catholic Church,
the communion of Saints,
the forgiveness of sins,
the resurrection of the body,
and life everlasting. Amen.

The Priest blows upon the Catechumen and touches the head, chest, and back with oil and chrism. The Priest says:

I anoint you with sanctified oil in the name of the Father, and of the Son, and of the Holy Spirit.

People: **Amen.**

Priest: Do you renounce Satan?

People: **I renounce him.**

Priest: And all his works?

People: **I renounce them.**

Priest: And all his pomps?

People: **I renounce them.**

Priest: We pray you, O LORD Holy Father, Almighty and Eternal God, have mercy on your servant, N., whom you have called to the beginning of Faith. Expel all blindness of the heart, break the snares of Satan by which your servant was bound, and open the door of your Truth. Clothe your servant with the +Sign of your Wisdom so that all foul desires may be avoided, being joyful in the sweet fragrance of your commandments. May this person serve you in the Church and make progress day by day that your servant may become sufficient to the promise of your grace; in the name of the Father, and of the Son, and of the Holy Spirit, now and ever, and unto the ages of ages.

Amen.

Prayer for a Sick Catechumen

I beg your healing, O LORD, Holy Father, Almighty and eternal God, who aids those in times of danger and tempers the scourges: We humbly pray to you, O LORD, that by your holy visitation, you raise your servant N. from this infirmity; place a limit on this trial, as you did for Job, and do not let the enemy triumph over this soul without the redemption of Baptism; O LORD, delay the outcome of death and extend this life; reveal whom you are leading towards the Sacrament of Baptism, so that the redeemed one is not harmed by your judgment; take away any opportunity for the devil to triumph and preserve those whom you have made ready to enjoin the Triumphant ones of Christ, so that your healed servant is reborn in your Church by the grace of Baptism; we ask this through LORD Jesus Christ, who reigns with you and the Holy Spirit, now and ever, and unto the ages of ages.

Amen.

The Exhortation

Let it not escape your notice, O Satan, that punishment is looming for you, that eternal torment is waiting for you on the day of judgment, the day of eternal punishment. That day is coming like a burning fire, where you and your angels face eternal destruction; therefore, for your wickedness you are damned and doomed. Give honor to the living God, give honor to Jesus Christ, and give honor to the Holy Spirit the Paraclete, in whose power I command you, whatever unclean spirit you may be, to leave and depart from these servants of God and restore them to their God, whom our LORD Jesus Christ has called to his grace and blessing, so that they may become his temple through the waters of regeneration for the remission of all sins; in the name of our LORD Jesus Christ, who will judge the living and the dead and the world by fire.

Amen.

Salt is placed into the mouth of the Catechumen.

"Effeta," which means "be opened," is an invocation in honor of pleasantness in the name of God the Father, the Son, and the Holy Spirit.

Priest: O LORD, Holy Father, Almighty and everlasting God, who is, who was, and who is to come, and who shall remain unto the end, whose beginning is unknown and whose end is incomprehensible; we humbly call upon you to help this servant, N., whom you have freed from the error of the Gentiles and their vile behavior; be pleased to hear this person humble oneself before you and be allowed to approach the font of Baptism; let your servant be renewed by water and the Holy Spirit, stripped of the old person and clothed with the new, created according to your likeness; may your servant assume the incorrupt and spotless vestment, and be found worthy to serve you, our LORD; in the name of our LORD Jesus Christ, who will judge the living and the dead and the world by fire.

People: **Amen.**

Priest: O God, who established the greatest Sacrament for the salvation of humanity in the substance of water: Be responsive to our invocation, and pour out your blessings upon this element of your manifold purification; Let this creature serve your mystery, and become effective for casting out demons and expelling diseases by your divine grace; Let it work so that whatever it touches or wherever it is sprinkled in the homes of the faithful may be free from impurity and released from harm; Do not let the presence of pestilent spirits remain nor any corrupting air; May all the hidden snares of the enemy be removed, and whatever opposes the safety or tranquility of the inhabitants may flee with the sprinkling of this water; May the health sought through the invocation of your name be protected from all attack; through Christ our LORD who reigns with you and the Holy Spirit, now and ever, and unto the ages of ages.

People: **Amen.**

Priest: Hear us O LORD, Holy Father, Almighty and everlasting God: Be pleased to send your holy angel from heaven, to watch over, support, protect, visit, and defend all who inhabit this dwelling, your servant; through Christ our LORD who reigns with you and the Holy Spirit, now and ever, and unto the ages of ages.

People: **Amen.**

The Catechumen is anointed with oil and chrism on the chest and shoulder blades before being baptized. The Priest and people chants the following litany around the font:

Priest: O God, make speed to save us.

People: **O LORD, make haste to help us.**

Priest: Glory be to the Father, and to the Son, and the Holy Spirit, as it was, as it is, as it shall be through the ages of ages. **Amen.**

Priest: We have sinned, O LORD, we have sinned, spare us our sins, and save us; you who guided Noah over the flood waves, hear us; who with your word recalled Jonah from the abyss, deliver us; who stretched forth your hand to Peter as he sank, help us, O Christ. Son of God, you accomplished marvelous things of the LORD with our fathers, be favorable in our days also; Stretch forth your hand from on high.

Priest: Deliver us, O Christ.

People: **Hear us, O Christ.**

Priest: Hear us, O Christ.

People: **Hear us, O LORD have mercy.**

Priest: Son of God, you who did marvelous things of the LORD with our fathers, be favorable in our days also; Stretch forth your hand from on high. Deliver us, O Christ.

People: **Hear us, O Christ.**
Saint Mary, **pray for us.**
Saint Peter, **pray for us.**
Saint Paul, **pray for us.**
Saint Andrew, **pray for us.**
Saint James, **pray for us.**
Saint Bartholomew, **pray for us.**

Saint Thomas, **pray for us.**

Saint Matthew, **pray for us.**

Saint James, **pray for us.**

Saint Madianus, **pray for us.**

Saint Mark, **pray for us.**

Saint Luke, **pray for us.**

All the Holy Saints, **pray for us.**

Exorcism of the Font

Priest: I exorcise you, O creature of water, through the living God, through the holy God: Who in the beginning separated you from the dry land by His word; whose Spirit was moving over you; who commanded you to flow out of paradise and to water the whole earth in four rivers; who brought you forth from the rock to quench the thirst of the people whom He had freed from Egypt; who sweetened your bitterness by wood.

I exorcise you through Jesus Christ His Son, who turned you into wine as a marvelous sign at Cana of Galilee; who walked upon you and was baptized by John in the Jordan; who brought you forth along with blood from His side, and commanded His disciples, saying, 'Go forth and teach all nations, baptizing them in the name of the Father, and of the Son, and of the Holy Spirit.'"

Therefore, I command you, every unclean spirit, every phantom, every deception of the spirit, to be eliminated and driven away from this creature of water, so that it may become a source of living water flowing forth unto eternal life; let this be made holy water, blessed water, for the regeneration of the children of God the Father Almighty, in the name of our LORD Jesus Christ, who is coming in the Holy Spirit to judge the world by fire.

People: **Amen.**

Priest: I exorcise you, O creature of water, in the name of God the Father Almighty, and in the name of our LORD Jesus Christ, His Son, and the Holy Spirit: I command every power of the adversary, every attack of the devil, and every phantom to be eliminated and driven away from this creature of water, so that it may be a fountain flowing forth unto eternal life; that whoever is baptized with it will become a temple of the living God unto the remission of sins; in the name of our LORD Jesus Christ, who will judge the living and the dead and the world by fire.

People: **Amen.**

Priest: Almighty and everlasting God, of your great mercy: Be present in your mysteries and in the sacraments; send forth the spirit of adoption to create new people whom the baptismal font labors to give birth into you; that what is done by our humble ministry is made complete with the power of your grace; through Christ our LORD who reigns with you and the Holy Spirit, now and ever, and unto the ages of ages.

People: **Amen.**

Priest: O God, who works miraculously through the unseen power of your Sacraments: Though we are unworthy to receive such great mysteries, do not withhold the gifts of your grace; incline your ears to our prayers, by the mercy of your kindness; through Christ our LORD who reigns with you and the Holy Spirit, now and ever, and unto the ages of ages.

People: **Amen.**

Priest: O God, whose spirit moved over the waters in the beginning of the world, so that even then the nature of water might receive the power of sanctification; O God, who washed away the reproach of the innocents of the world through the waters, thus signaling the pattern of regeneration through the flood, with the ministry of one and the same element both to end pollution and begin virtuous life: Look upon your Church and multiply in her your generations; by your overflowing grace, gladden your city and open the baptismal font to renew the nations throughout the earth; By the command of your majesty, may it receive the grace of your only-begotten Son by the Holy Spirit, who enriches this water prepared for the regeneration of humanity by the admixture of His illumination; let this sanctified water bring forth a new creation from the immaculate womb of the divine font, so that those who are distinguished by gender in body or age in time may all be born from one mother by grace.

Therefore, let all unclean spirits depart from this place and all diabolical delusions cease; let nothing contrary to virtue inhabit this place, nor any deceitful spirit lurk or corrupt by contamination; let this holy and innocent creature be free from all assault, purified by the expulsion of all wickedness, and be a living and regenerating fountain, a purifying water, so that all who are cleansed by this saving bath, through of the Holy Spirit, may obtain the perfect purification and forgiveness; through Christ our LORD who reigns with you and the Holy Spirit, now and ever, and unto the ages of ages.

People: **Amen.**

Priest: Therefore I bless you, O creature of water, by God the Father, by the Holy God, who in the beginning separated you from the dry land by His Word and commanded that the whole earth be watered by four rivers; who for the thirsty people in the desert made you sweet and potable, brought forth from the rock: I bless you through Jesus Christ, His only Son, our LORD, who by His marvelous sign, turned you into wine at Cana of Galilee; who walked upon you and was baptized in you by John in the Jordan; who said that believers should be baptized in you, saying, 'Go, teach all nations, baptizing them in the name of the Father, and of the Son, and of the Holy Spirit.'

O Almighty God, may you be present to us who keep your commandments: In your clemency, may you breathe upon these simple waters and bless them with your mouth, so that in addition to the natural cleansing they provide for bodies, that they may also be effective for purifying souls; may the power of your Spirit descend into the fullness of this font, and the entire substance of this water be fruitful for regeneration, so that here the stains of all sins may be wiped away; may this nature be cleansed as in your image, so that every person who enters this sacrament of regeneration may be reborn into the true innocence of a new infancy; through Christ our LORD who reigns with you and the Holy Spirit, now and ever, and unto the ages of ages.

People: **Amen.**

Alternative Exorcism of the Font

Priest: I exorcise you, unclean spirit, through God the Father almighty, who made heaven and earth, the sea, and all that is in them; that every power of the adversary, every works of the devil, every attack, every phantasm of the enemy, may be eliminated and expelled from this creature of water, that it may be holy and benefi-cial, and like a burning fire turned against the snares of the enemy, through the invocation of the name of our LORD Jesus Christ, who will judge the world by fire, in the Holy Spirit.

People: **Amen.**

As the hart panteth after the fountains of water; so my soul pan-teth after thee, O God. My soul hath thirsted after the strong living God; when shall I come and appear before the face of God? *Psalm 42: 2-3*

Bring to the LORD, O ye children of God: bring to the LORD the offspring of rams. Bring to the LORD glory and honour: bring to the LORD glory to his name: adore ye the LORD in his holy court. The voice of the LORD is upon the waters; the God of majesty hath thundered, The LORD is upon many waters. *Psalm 23:1-3*

Once the blessing is completed, the priest places chrism into the font in the form of a cross, and whoever wishes can fill a small vessel with the blessed water to consecrate their homes. The people present are sprinkled with holy water.

Baptism of the Catechumen

Deacon: Do you believe in God the Almighty Father?

Person: **I believe.**

Deacon: Do you believe in Jesus Christ, His Only-Begotten Son, our LORD, who was born and suffered?

Person: **I believe.**

Deacon: Do you believe also in the Holy Spirit, the catholic church, the forgiveness of sins, and the resurrection of the body?

Person: **I believe.**

The Catechumen descends into the font and is immersed three times or asperged. After being baptized, he is anointed with chrism on the forehead, and the deacon places a white vestment on his head.

The Chrismation

Priest: God Almighty, Father of our LORD Jesus Christ, who has regenerated you by water and the Holy Spirit, has granted you the remission of all your sins. May He anoint you with the chrism of salvation in Christ.Top of Form

The one who is baptized is anointed with Holy Chrism here.

Priest: I anoint you with the oil and chrism of salvation and sanctification, in the name of God the Father, and of the Son, and of the Holy Spirit, now and ever, and unto the ages of ages.

People: **Amen.**

Priest: Work, O creature of oil: Work in the name of God the Almighty Father, and of the Son, and of the Holy Spirit, so that no unclean spirit may be hidden here, neither in the limbs, nor in the marrow, nor in the joints, but may the power of Christ, the Son of the living God, the Most High, and the Holy Spirit, work within you throughout all ages of ages.

People: **Amen.**

The Deacon places a white vestment over his/her head. The Priest says:

Priest: Receive this white vestment, holy and unblemished, which you may wear before the judgment of our LORD Jesus Christ.

Person: **I accept it and wear it.**

Priest: Receive the + sign of the cross of Christ in your right hand, and may it keep you for eternal life.

Person: **Amen.**

The Mandatum

His feet are washed and a towel is given to dry them. This is followed by a liturgical chant or series of phrases:

Choir and People: **Alleluia, your word is a lamp to my feet, O LORD.**
Alleluia, help me, O LORD, and I will be saved.
Alleluia, visit us, O LORD, with your salvation.
Alleluia, you have commanded your commandments to be kept greatly.

You have commanded your mercy, do not neglect the work of your hands. If I, your LORD and Teacher, have washed your

feet, you ought to wash each other's feet. For I have given you an example, that just as I have done, you should do to others.

Priest: Our LORD and Savior Jesus Christ, on the day before he suffered, took a clean and immaculate towel, girded his loins, poured water into a basin, and washed His disciples' feet. So should you do, following the example of our LORD Jesus Christ, to your guests and pilgrims.

The First Communion

Priest: May the Body and Blood of our LORD Jesus Christ be for you into eternal life.

People: **Amen.**

Priest: Nourished with the spiritual food, and renewed with the heavenly sustenance of the Body and Blood of the LORD: Let us give due praise and thanks to God, our LORD Jesus Christ, praying for His unfailing mercy so that the sacrament of this divine gift may lead to the increase of faith and progress towards eternal salvation; through Christ our LORD who reigns with you and the Holy Spirit, now and ever, and unto the ages of ages.

People: **Amen.**

Priest: Let us pray, beloved brothers and sisters, for our brother N., who has received the grace of the LORD, that he may carry the received baptism unblemished and whole before the judgment seat of our LORD Jesus Christ, who reigns with you and the Holy Spirit, now and ever, and unto the ages of ages.

People: **Amen.**

Priest: We give you thanks, O God, through whom we have celebrated this Holy Mystery and from whom we ask for the gift of your sanctification; through our LORD Jesus Christ, who reigns with you and the Holy Spirit, now and ever, and unto the ages of ages.

People: **Amen.**

Choir and People: **Alleluia, remember us, O LORD according to the favor of your people; visit us with your salvation.**

Alleluia, O LORD, make us safe; O LORD, grant us prosperity.

Alleluia, show us, O LORD, your mercy.

Priest: Save us, O Jesus who can save, who gave life and salvation: our LORD Jesus Christ, who reigns with you and the Holy Spirit, now and ever, and unto the ages of ages.

People: **Amen.**

The Priest signs the new communicant, saying:

Priest: You are marked with the seal of the cross of Christ. Peace be with you forever.

People: **Amen.**

Order of Visitation of the Sick

The following liturgical text is provided conditionally that the sick or infirmed person is capable of speech, or multiple people are present. If this individual is alone and cannot speak, then the Priest will pray the entire service.

Ministry of the Word

Priest: Brothers and sisters, let us pray to the LORD our God for our brother N., who is afflicted by the cruelty of this present illness: With the mercy of the LORD, who gave life and salvation, may He deign to heal with heavenly medicine; through Christ our LORD who reigns with you and the Holy Spirit, now and ever, and unto the ages of ages.

Person: **Amen.**

Priest: O living and Almighty God, who is quick to restore and strengthen all works: Beloved brothers and sisters, let us humbly pray for our sick brother N., so that the creature may feel the hand of the Creator, either in restoration or recovery, that the merciful Father may graciously renew His work in His Name; through Christ our LORD who reigns with you and the Holy Spirit, now and ever, and unto the ages of ages.

Person: **Amen.**

Priest: Holy LORD, Father of all things, Almighty author of eternal life in whom all things live; who revives the dead and calls into existence things that are not, becoming like those that are; who is the great builder: Exercise mercy upon your creation; through

Christ our LORD who reigns with you and the Holy Spirit, now and ever, and unto the ages of ages.

Person: **Amen.**

Priest: Beloved brothers and sisters, let us beseech God in whose hand is the living, who is the life of the dying: Heal the weakness of this body and to grant salvation to the soul, so that what does not deserve mercy by its own merit may attain the grace of mercy through our prayers; through Christ our LORD who reigns with you and the Holy Spirit, now and ever, and unto the ages of ages.

Person: **Amen.**

Priest: Holy LORD, Father Almighty and everlasting God, who is the way, the truth, and the life: Hear and preserve your servant N., whom you have enlivened and redeemed by the great and precious holy Blood of your Son, who reigns with you and the Holy Spirit, now and ever, and unto the ages of ages.

Person: **Amen.**

Priest: O God, who desires not the death of a sinner, but that he be converted and may live: Grant the forgiveness of sins in this one whose heart turned from you, and bestow the grace of eternal life; through Christ our LORD who reigns with you and the Holy Spirit, now and ever, and unto the ages of ages.

Person: **Amen.**

Priest: O God, who with loving affection always offers yourself for your creation: Incline your ear to us as we supplicate for your servant N., afflicted by the adversity of bodily illness; look upon him with a gentle gaze, visit him in your salvation, and grant him the heavenly medicine of divine grace; through Christ our LORD who reigns with you and the Holy Spirit, now and ever, and unto the ages of ages.

Person: **Amen.**

Gospel Reading

Matt. 22:23; 29-33

That day there came to him the Sadducees, who say there is no resurrection; and asked him, And Jesus answering, said to them: You err, not knowing the Scriptures, nor the power of God. For in the resurrection they shall neither marry nor be married; but shall be as the angels of God in heaven. And concerning the resurrection of the dead, have you not read that which was spoken by God, saying to you: I am the God of Abraham, and the God of Isaac, and the God of Jacob? He is not the God of the dead, but of the living. And the multitudes hearing it, were in admiration at his doctrine.

Holy Unction

The Priest dips a thumb in the holy oil, and makes a sign of the cross on the sick person's forehead, saying:

I anoint you with sanctified oil, that you may recover your health, in the Name of the Father, and of the Son, and of the Holy Spirit, now and ever, and unto the ages of ages. **Amen.**

Priest: O LORD, grant us your servants, that with confidence we may be worthy to pray:

Person: **Our Father in heaven, hallowed be your name; your kingdom come, your will be done, on earth as it is in heaven. Give us today our substantial bread. Forgive us our debts as we forgive our debtors. Keep us from falling into temptation and deliver us from evil.**

Priest: For yours is the kingdom, and the power, and the glory of the Father, and the Son, and Holy Spirit, now and ever, and unto the ages of ages.

Person: **Amen.**

Priest: Deliver us, O LORD, from all evil and guard us in all good, O Jesus Christ, the source of all goodness, who reigns with you and the Holy Spirit, now and ever, and unto the ages of ages. *Person:* **Amen.**

Priest: We pray to you, O LORD, for our brother N., that if any secular stain attacks him, or any worldly vice has afflicted him in his infirmity, that he may be forgiven and cleansed by your mercy; through Christ our LORD who reigns with you and the Holy Spirit, now and ever, and unto the ages of ages.

Person: **Amen.**

Priest: O LORD, holy Father, we fervently beseech you that by the reception of this most holy Eucharist of the body and blood of our LORD Jesus Christ, that for both the health of body and soul of our brother may be made well; through Christ our LORD who reigns with you and the Holy Spirit, now and ever, and unto the ages of ages.

Person: **Amen.**

Priest: O LORD Jesus Christ, our God, hear us as we pray for our sick brother, that your holy Eucharist may be his/her protection; through Christ our LORD who reigns with you and the Holy Spirit, now and ever, and unto the ages of ages.

Person: **Amen.**

Holy Communion

Priest: May the peace and love of our LORD Jesus Christ, and the communion of his Saints, be always with us.

Person: **Amen.**

The Eucharist is offered from the reserved Sacrament, the Priest saying:

May the Body and Blood of our LORD Jesus Christ, Son of the living and Most High God, be with you forever. **Amen.**

Priest: Having received our salvific nourishment of the divine Body, let us give thanks to our LORD Jesus Christ; through the Sacrament of his Body and Blood, has delivered us from death and deigned to give a medicine to humanity for both body and soul; who reigns with you and the Holy Spirit, now and ever, and unto the ages of ages.

Person: **Amen.**

Priest: We give thanks to God the Father Almighty, that by the gift of His Sacrament, has transformed us from our earthly origin and nature into the heavenly nature; through Christ our LORD who reigns with you and the Holy Spirit, now and ever, and unto the ages of ages.

Person: **Amen.**

Convert us, O God of our salvation, and grant us the salvation of our infirmities, for he has satisfied the longing soul and the hungry soul he has filled with goodness. Alleluia, alleluia. *Psalm 104:9*

Visit us, O God, with your salvation. Alleluia. *Psalm 105:4*

You are my strength unto salvation. Alleluia. *Psalm 117:14*

I will take the cup of salvation, and I will call upon the name of the LORD. Alleluia. *Psalm 115:13*

Refreshed by the body and blood of Christ, may we always say to you, LORD. Alleluia.

Offer sacrifices of righteousness, and trust in the LORD. *Psalm 4:6*

Priest: We give you thanks, O God, through whom we have celebrated the Holy Mysteries and from whom we seek the gifts of sanctity; who reigns with you and the Holy Spirit, now and ever, and unto the ages of ages.

Person: **Amen.**

Benediction

The service concludes with the following dismissal

May the LORD bless you and keep you; may the LORD reveal his face to you and have mercy on you; may the LORD turn his countenance towards you and give you peace. **Amen.**

The Priest makes a sign of the cross with his right hand, saying:

You are marked with the +Sign of the Cross of Christ. Peace be with you forever. **Amen.**

Rubrics for Ordinary Mass

FOR THE PROPER CELEBRATION of Mass, it is necessary for the Celebrant—most likely the Priest—to have a set of instructions on how Mass is traditionally conducted. These instructions, or rubrics, are necessary for the Priest but may also provide some theological instruction to laity. For example, each element has an important role during the celebration of Mass where symbolism is applied to them based on theological principles. Within the chancel, the Altar represents the persecution that was inflicted. The chalice represents the Church that has been established on the persecution and martyrdom of the Prophets and others (*et aliorum*).[1]

The prayers and hymns that are sung within the Mass, from the introit to the Epistle and Gradual, represents the law of Nature to which the knowledge of Christ has renewed every communicant and their deeds. However, from the Epistle and Gradual to uncovering the Chalice is a commemoration of the law of Moses to which Christ has been prophesied but has not Incarnated. These representations create a nuanced and complex series of symbolic associations wherein the removal of a single element entails a deficiency within the entire liturgy. Therefore, everything contained within the Mass must be given due care and prudent consideration.

When the Priest is celebrating the Mass, he is standing in front of the Altar facing away from the people (*ante altare*) with extended hands.[2] This was a common prayer posture in both Eastern and Western Christianity, which would naturally be part of Gaelic tradition. While the Priest was facing away from the people

---

1. This segment was moved from its original location for the sake of procedure. See Stowe Missal, 40.

2. See Warren, Liturgy and Ritual, 111.

throughout the Mass, the praying posture was used particularly during the consecration of the elements. Throughout the Mass, the prayers are either sung using Gregorian chant or said aloud if the Priest is not trained in this tradition.

Introit and Vesting

The initial liturgical action is the entrance rite or *introit*, where the Bishop or Priest enters the nave and approaches the Altar. The entire introit is sung antiphonally between the Priest and the choir; if the parish does not have a choir, then the responses may be sung by the congregation. [3] A psalm appointed for the day may be sung by the choir antiphonally and in Gregorian chant, or by the people depending on the parish.

Once the introit is complete, and the Priest and Deacon have entered into the chancel, they begin donning their vestments. Within the Lorrha Missal there is a vesting prayer for the Priest, consisting of several discrete prayers that the Priest sings to bless his vestments. This includes a chausible, alb, maniple, metal bracelets or cuffs of silk, and a cassock or caracalla. However, Bishops were more ornate and wore a rationale, ring and brooch symbolizing episcopal authority, a pectoral cross, and crown[4] with a pastoral staff. The vesting prayers are as follows:

Prayer for the alb

Priest: O God of Sabaoth, Most High, Holy Father, be pleased to gird me with the tunic of chastity.

Prayer for the cinture

Priest: Gird my loins with the cinture of love of you.

---

3. It is also possible for the entire introit to be sung by one chorister, and the Gloria patri to be sung by the congregation. See Tietze, Hymn Introits, 34.

4. It is documented that Bishops wore golden crowns instead of mitres, as they were not introduced until the 10th century. See Warren, Liturgy and Ritual, 120.

Aifreann na hÉireann

Prayer for the stole

Priest: And inflame the loins of my heart with the fire of your charity.

Prayer for the right cuff

Priest: So that I can make an intercession for my sins.

Prayer for the left cuff

Priest: And earn the remission of the sins of those present.

Prayer for the maniple

Priest: And sacrifice the peaceable offerings of each one."[5]

The Prayer of St. Augustine is then sung or said, to which the Priest offers incense over the covered Host and Chalice. Once the collects after the Litany have been sung, the Chalice and Host are uncovered by half. With their partial uncovering, the Priest offers the following prayer three times with incense. The linen cloth is then lifted from the Chalice with another prayer sung three times. The Gospel and Alleluia, so far as the oblatory prayers, are a commemoration of the law of the Prophets who predicted the Incarnation.

Uncovering and Elevation

After the recitation of the Symbol, the Chalice is fully uncovered and elevated with the singing of the offering (*quando canitur oblata*). This act is a commemoration of Christ's birth and of His glory through signs and miracles. When the Host is elevated above the Altar (*super altare*)—representing the turtle-dove—the Priest says, "Jesus Christ, Alpha and Omega, who is the beginning and the

---

5. This prayer was removed from the Mass text, as it was deemed to be better suited for clerical instruction.

end" (*Iesus Christus, Alpha et Omega, hoc est principium et finis*). This represents Christ's Body which has been set in the linen sheet of the Virgin Mary's womb.[6]

When the Elevation prayers are said, the Priest bows three time in repentance of his sins. He offers the Chalice to God, saying "O God, have mercy on me." The people kneel in silence, so that it may not disturb the priest and separate his mind from God. For this reason, it is referred to as the perilous prayer (*periculosa oratio*). The Priest then takes three steps backwards and then steps forward, representing the triad in which everyone sins in thought, word, and deed. This also represents the triad of things by which he is renewed and moved to Christ's Body.

To prepare for the submersion of the Host, the Priest must first consecrate and prepare the water and wine. The Priest first pours the water in the chalice (*in calicem*), saying "I beseech you, Father, I implore you, Son, I beg you, Holy Spirit" (*Peto te, Pater, deprecor te, Fili, obsecro te, Spiritus Sancte*). This represents the people that have been poured into the Church. He then pours wine into the water-bearing chalice, representing the pouring of Christ's divinity on His humanity and on the people at Baptism. The Priest then says, "The Father forgives, the Son grants indulgence, the Holy Spirit offers mercy" (*Remittit Pater, indulget Filius, miseretue Spiritus Sanctus*).[7]

Examination

After the priest prays for the LORD's mercy to descend upon the people, he examines the chalice and host with the intention of determining how to break the latter. This symbolizes the insults, assault, and capture of Christ, where the host on the paten is Christ's flesh on the Cross. Once the prayer is complete, the Host is fractured representing the breaking of Christ's Body being nailed onto the Cross. The two halves of the Host are then submerged and then

6. This segment was moved from its original location for the sake of procedure. See Stowe Missal, 40.

7. ibid.

brought together, representing the submersion and wholeness of His Body in His Blood after His crucifixion.

A particle is then separated from the bottom-left corner of the Host, representing Christ being wounded with the Spear of Longinus in the right armpit. As Christ was facing westward away from the people (*contra civitatem*), and eastward was the face of Longinus. This symbolism places Longinus on the left with Christ on the right.

Confraction

The Confraction is done in seven distinct ways: the division into five particles representing the five senses; seven for the host of Saints and Virgins except for the chief ones; eight with the separated particle representing the nine households of heaven and grades of the Church; eleven representing the incomplete number of Apostles after the betrayal of Judas; twelve representing the first day of the month, Circumcision, and Maundy Thursday, and in commemoration of the Apostles; thirteen representing either Low Sunday and Festival of the Ascension, or Christ with His Apostles.

The summation of these particles—five, seven, eight, nine, eleven, twelve, and thirteen—total sixty-five, the number of particles reserved for Easter, Christmas, Whitsunday. These particles represent the totality of Christ, taking the shape of a Cross in the paten where the upper part is inclined on the Priest's left hand. This represents the bowing of Christ's head and the surrendering of his spirit (*inclinatio capite tradidit spiritum*).

The configuration of these particles on Easter and Christmas consists of thirteen particles in the stem of the Cross, nine in the crosspiece, twenty in the circle-wheel, five for each angle, sixteen in both the circle and body of the cross, or four for each angle. In ideal circumstances, the middle particle is reserved for the Priest, representing the secrets held in his heart. The particles going upwards to the shaft belongs to the Bishop. The crosspiece is reserved for the anchorites and penitents. The upper left and right angles are reserved for young clerics and innocent children respectively.

The lower left and right angles are reserved for repentant people and those lawfully married.

Communion and Benediction

The celebration of Holy Communion was referred to by many names within the Gaelic tradition, including but not limited to "Offering" (offerre), "Holy Offering" (*sacra offerre*), and "Sacrificial Offering" (*sacraficium offerre*).[8] The term sacraficium possessed a dual meaning, referencing that which is offered to God and what is offered to the communicant. These titles not only point to the sacred act of communion among fellow believers but is deeply entrenched with theology related to the presence of Christ within the elements.

When receiving Communion, it is important to be mindful of the representations and symbols found within the Mass. It is particularly important to be mindful that the portion of the Host that one receives is a bodily member of Christ Crucified, and that there may be a cross of labor according to the communicant through union with the crucified Body. For this reason, it is imprudent to swallow one's particle without tasting it as it is improper to not appreciate the experience of these Holy Mysteries. It is also improper to consume it using one's back teeth, as it represents the imprudent disputes over the Holy Mysteries that may lead to heresy.[9]

The Priest will offer a benediction with his right hand, to which his first, second, and fourth fingers are extended with the thumb covering the third finger over the palm.[10] This gesture may also be used during the consecration, fraction, and submersion of the Host by the Bishop or at the discretion of the Priest.

---

8. This one is particularly noteworthy, as it was the name used by St. Gall while giving his student Magnoaldus a lecture. St. Gall was recorded as the student of St. Columbanus. See Warren, Liturgy and Ritual, 95.

9. Stowe Missal, 42.

10. The Priest may also offer the benediction with the thumb, index, and middle finger extended, and the third and fourth fingers curled into his hand. See Warren, Liturgy and Ritual, 100.

Bibliography

Breen, Aidan. "The Text of the Constantinopolitan Creed in the Stowe Missal." *Proceedings of the Royal Irish Academy: Archaeology, Culture, History, Literature* 90C, (1990): 107–121.

Heller, Dagmar and Hanne Lamparter. "Worship and Spirituality." In *Christianity in Western and Northern Europe*, edited by Todd M. Johnson, Annemarie C Mayer, and Kenneth R. Ross. Edinburgh: Edinburgh University, 2024.

Hen, Yitzhak. "The Liturgy of the Irish on the Continent." In *The Irish in Early Medieval Europe: Identity, Culture and Religion*, edited by Roy Flechner and Sven Meeder. London: Palgrave, 2016.

Hunwicke, J.W. "Kerry and Stowe Revisited." *Proceedings of the Royal Irish Academy: Archaeology, Culture, History, Literature* 102C, No. 1 (2002): 1–19.

Meeder, Sven. "The Early Irish Stowe Missal's Destination and Function." *Early Medieval Europe* 13, No. 2 (2005): 179–194.

Nooij, Lars B. "A New History of the Stowe Missal: Towards an Edition of the Stowe John and the Irish Tract on the Mass." PhD diss. Maynooth University, 2021.

Ryan, John. "The Sacraments in the Early Irish Church." *Irish Quarterly Review* 51, No. 204 (1962): 371–384.

Stevenson, Jane Barbara. "Monastic Rules of Columbanus." In *Columbanus: Studies on the Latin Writings, Volume 17*, edited by Michael Lapidge. Woodbridge: Boydell, 1997.

Tietze, Christoph. *Hymn Introits for the Liturgical Year: The Origin and Early Development of the Latin Texts*. Batesville: Hillenbrand, 2007.

The Stowe Missal, edited by George F. Warner. London: Harrison and Sons, 1915.

Warren, F.E. *The Liturgy and Ritual of the Celtic Church*. Oxford: Clarendon, 1881.

www.ingramcontent.com/pod-product-compliance
Ingram Content Group UK Ltd.
Pitfield, Milton Keynes, MK11 3LW, UK
UKHW020952100325
4920UKWH00032B/280

9 798385 235698